AF539470

# THE WOUNDED WORLD

# THE WOUNDED WORLD

## Essays on Ethics and Politics

Saitya Brata Das

THE WOUNDED WORLD: Essays on Ethics and Politics
Saitya Brata Das



First Published, 2013

ISBN : 978-93-5002-245-0



*Published by*
**AAKAR BOOKS**
28 E Pocket IV, Mayur Vihar Phase I, Delhi 110 091
Phone : 011 2279 5505 Telefax : 011 2279 5641
info@aakarbooks.com; www.aakarbooks.com

*Printed at*
Mudrak, 30 A, Patparganj, Delhi 110 091

*For Sarita and Mrinmay*

# *Acknowledgements*

The publication of this book financially benefits from the University Grants Commission under the Special Assistance Programme. I wish to thank my colleagues at the Centre for English Studies, School of Language, Literature and Culture Studies of Jawaharlal Nehru University, especially Prof. G.J.V. Prasad and Prof. Saugata Bhaduri for making this possible. I thank Mr. K.K. Saxena of Aakar Books for bringing out this book in such a short time and for bringing to me, once again, the deepest and the most beautiful experience of seeing a book published and the happiness that, after all, there has not yet been a complete victory of the darkness of oblivion. Then there is Sarita and Mrinmay, my little darling, to offer my thanks. This book is a humble gift to these two lovely people in my life.

# *Contents*

# *Introduction*

## I

This book consists of 11 essays written over 13 years, all of them —apart from the essay on Martin Heidegger's theologico-political question—were written for conferences or for talks delivered on various occasions in various places. The first essay is the very last, according to the dates of their composition, and the last is the first born among them. They, therefore, bear the birthmark of their time. The author has not taken much labour to bring fundamental transformation in the substance of these essays, apart from correcting some minor grammatical mistakes and making their arguments clearer. No attempt has been made to make them "up-to-date" or to make them appear "recent", not because they are considered to be some great works with "untimely" values, but rather because the author perceives that a position that was dear to him once, a strategy that was once undertaken, a move that was made once, an event that he has received in the youth of his thinking—even though it is now left behind long ago—retains its own validity in so far as its birth appears to be necessary in a retrospective gaze, in so far as each one was born unique and thus bears the singular tear and wear of its time. One must not neglect or undermine the achievement or dream of one's youth—as Adorno remarked once—even though it appears, in the retrospective look, that the moment of beginning is far from fulfilment and that it is more like groping in the darkness with sudden flashes of lightning appearing at opportune moments only to disappear the next moment. To respect the dream of one's youth demands respecting the singularity of arrival—of these flashes of lightning, of these aleatory events of thought that have arrived at their own time without ever being possessed by the thinker or the writer. He is the only one who offers himself as a site where something like this may happen. To allow something like this to happen at all, to let oneself be the site for the event of thinking to manifest at all, can be the highest task of a thinker. Each event of thought has its own memory and own mode of forgetting; each one bears its own tear and wear. While it appears and disappears in its own mode of coming and going, it leaves behind traces, more invisible than visible, the more invisible the more visible it is to us, traces that make the inner life of a thinker a kind of secret to himself and to the light of the world, withdrawn from the luminosity of knowledge, concealed from the intelligibility of cognition. They thereby preserve themselves from the violence of cognition, waiting to manifest at opportune moments when the world seems to arrive at a sudden halt. Nothing is more enigmatic to me than this secret of life which is the life of a thinker, nourished by these events of thought, by these momentary lightning flashes of truth when life becomes almost indistinguishable from truth, or when life almost touches death, barely separated by a hair's breath. It is enigmatic how a fundamental encounter with truth invisibly transforms the whole inner being of a thinker which is a revolutionary moment, singularizing him in respect to himself and to the whole world around him. One must, therefore, respect the immanent transiency of this life and of these events, which is also their eternity and their immortality: while they can be arranged according to the "dates" of their arrival in the clock-time of composition, their real-truth time has something like an inescapable air of eternity around them. In that sense, youth is to be considered as nothing other than this most acute exposure to the unnameable and the overwhelming, that is, this impossible experience of eternity and of time, if eternity is nothing other than the very source of time itself. There is, as if, a nobility and beauty of transiency that, in its passing, prohibits violence of knowledge upon it. To withdraw from this violence is strenuous and the redemptive task of the discourse called "philosophy".

Therefore, these essays are not fundamentally transformed or "updated", for to do that would amount to force them speak in a language that was not yet born but only searched for in the darkness of presence. Or, rather, it was already as "not there". In this profound sense, for me, it is uncalled for a thinker to be anxious that his once written essay or his once arrived event of thought will soon become "out-dated" or "dated", for who is he to pass judgment on the (un)importance of his works for the time to come? I therefore caution myself all the time not to fall into this anxiety and this arrogance to pass judgment on one's own works and others, as much as possible. Thinking in the life of a thinker, since thinking never stops once this madness called "thinking" begins, has this immortality—a very old idea of philosophy—which does not need to oppose itself to transiency at all. It is rather nourished by the transient and abides in it.

## II

This collection of essays bears the title *The Wounded World*. It calls for an explanation. The title of a book is always a matter of decision. Since a creative title does not have and must not have the character of algorithm, it can only be seized in a manner that, in its very arrest-like character, communicates something like the "ethos" or atmosphere in which the thoughts to follow take their breath. It is the invisible *anima* of thought which is also the condition of their visibility as such that the title must seize upon. While being disparate for obvious reasons—they are occasional writings—these essays participate in a certain experience of finitude or transiency which marks the wound of the world, that which wounds the world, and which precisely thereby opens the world to the thinker. Thinking takes its birth at the moment of being wounded, the moment when the world suddenly becomes something like a wound, when life becomes a question mark, when nothing in the world appears to be so absolute and self-sufficient. It is a condition of abandonment, a non-condition rather, a desert of the world, of being left apart—disjoined from the totality of all relations—bereft of all consolation and satisfaction. It seems to be like a radical Godlessness, as it were, wherein a new opening to the divine may at all be possible one day. If there is no such wound, if the world as it exists is sufficient for the mortals, philosophy would be mere superfluous luxury, a pastime for the idle chatter, a prattle arising out of boredom. These essays, concerned as they are with questions of the ethical and the political, therefore take their point of departure from such an experience of transiency which is not at all closure of thought, but may open the essential thinking to take place at all. They arise from this experience of mortality that makes each thought singular, destined to incompletion and brokenness, bereft of the consolation which the Absolute alone can give to us. Hence these are to be called finite thoughts, and these ethical reflections may well be understood as exercises on a possible "ethics of finitude". As fissured by mortality, they are *tragic*. The tragic character of a finite thought is also a gesture, or the gesture of withdrawal par excellence, from all totalization by putting their hope elsewhere, by putting their stake in a future always *to come*. The tragic is that which singularizes—existence, thoughts, events, and the world. Not to shy away from the desert of the world, from the wound of life is the very adventure and promise of philosophy which it often allows itself to forget. The task of the following pages is nothing other than renewal of this promise and to undertake, once again, such an adventure of thought.

# *Affirmation of Deconstruction**

It is often heard that deconstruction, a singular manner, or a style or a gesture associated primarily with the French philosopher Jacques Derrida, is essentially an operation of negativity and a textual strategy of infinite reversal and displacement that renders any coherent meaning impossible. Consequently it may amount to a relativism or even nihilism of some sort, or, at worst, to a 'theory' of hair-splitting, brain storming play of words, albeit the most sophisticated one in recent years, that makes nullity of any serious and responsible ethico-political engagement. In this essay I hope to show that the profound importance of deconstruction for us lies rather in its infinite and unconditional affirmation of a justice to come, which is a messianic idea par excellence that in its unconditionality links itself with a certain experience of the impossible. Linking Derrida's thoughts with the works of Walter Benjamin and a few other philosophers, we argue that this affirmation of the unconditioned raises some very profound ethico-political questions for our time.

## I

We often hear that "deconstruction", which is supposed to be a "theory", a theory among other theories that literature students and

* This paper was presented at a conference on "Traditions of Intellectual Inquiry: Histories, Politics, Responses", at Lady Shri Ram College, Delhi University, March 22-23, 2013.

teachers in literature departments of universities are generally concerned with, a "theory" that is primarily associated with the French philosopher Jacques Derrida, is essentially a technical, a very complicated and sophisticated textual exercise of making the meaning of a text equivocal, ambivalent, undecidable and even impossible. We hear that deconstruction is a kind of Scepticism, a Cynicism, relativism or a form of nihilism that is bent on making nullity of everything, that irrefutable and self-refuting enemy of truth or even morality with any self-foundational claim. In other words, deconstruction which inherits *Destruktion*, "destruction" of Martin Heidegger is essentially a negative gesture. Philosophers and non-philosophers alike who hate such unbearable "jargon" from the depth of their hearts demand a more positive and constructive concept or idea so that infinite acts of negation may not end up hurling all that is beautiful and all that makes sense of life and the world into the abyss of destruction. Scholars who do "theory" are at once at unease with and even resist it with a certain repellence and yet desire it all the more thereby to involve themselves with this impossible and very complicated exercise of tearing apart of texts and of freeing the elements of play from the fixed centre of sobriety, for deconstruction supposed to have reduced everything into the textual universe of infinite traces and thereby leaving nothing outside the text. This desire, nourished by repellence, arises because deconstruction appears to be both the most un-theoretical and un-theorizable gesture, and yet, precisely thereby appears to be the most coveted "theory", being "sophisticated" and "hermetic", or even the aristocratic gesture par excellence. To read the works of Jacques Derrida anew and in a creative manner, when readings like the ones mentioned above have never ceased overdetermining his works for so many decades, is a difficult exercise, especially in our immediate academic context. This, however, necessitates that we undertake once again, that means always anew, such a task of reading. All reading, reading as such, in itself, is a responsibility, in so far as reading involves a response, an act of responding that releases that element of singularity from that which threatens petrification and obfuscation in overdetermination and thereby opening up the redemptive possibilities from the violence of cognition. In other words, reading is essentially a messianic gesture.

## II

First of all, to begin with, there is more than one manner or one way of affirming. There is an affirmation which belongs to the sphere of "assertive" and " positive" as against "negative". One asserts something; one posits something *as* something which is not-negative, or which rises and installs itself against the negative. The assertive or the positive affirmation is thus a conditioned or conditional affirmation; it affirms by an act of positing, by installing itself as "this" and not the "other". It is a thesis, a thetic act from which a certain originary context of violence is inseparable. This is, as we readers of Walter Benjamin know, is the originary guilt-context of mythic violence and is the origin of law which is two-fold—the law positing and law preserving violence (Benjamin 1986, pp. 277-300). Other than this, Benjamin affirms an unconditional and unconditioned divine violence, which is a strange violence in that it is violence without violence, without the violence of law, a violence 'without spilling blood' (Ibid., p. 297). This divine violence is another affirmation, another manner of affirming which is neither assertive nor positive and therefore is both *before* assertive and negative. In a beautiful essay devoted to Maurice Blanchot, Michel Foucault coins a felicitous phrase which I would like to borrow here, while being attentive to the singularity and difference between these different discourses. Foucault in this essay hints at an affirmation which is a *non-positive affirmation.* Such an affirmation does not need the positive and the assertive to affirm, for it affirms not something conditional but affirms itself—an affirmation of affirmation, affirmation that affirms itself (Foucault 1999, p. 74). We will soon see here that Derrida's affirmation is in close proximity to this Maurice Blanchot's non-positive affirmation, affirmation "before" the law, before assertion and before negation.

Hence affirmation is never unitary. There is always more than one manner and one way of saying "Yes". There is a "Yes" which is not a yes among other yes; therefore it is not "a" yes. It is not a number among numbers; it is not a measure among measures. It is *the immeasurable* par excellence and thus it is *singular*: the unrepeatable, aleatory event of affirmation, heterogeneous to all given conditions, to all calculability of knowledge and exceptional to the order of the normative. For Derrida, only the immeasurable is such Yes; or, only the Yes is the immeasurable, not because the Yes is dependent upon or conditioned by the immeasurable and vice-versa, but because the *Yes itself is the immeasurable and the immeasurable itself is the Yes. There is the Yes of an affirmation that is not measurable by any conditions, by any law, by making it a means to an end. It is rather an affirmation without means and also, thereby, without an end: Yes, a Yes and a Yes again.* In one of his most profound books, which also happens to be the most badly and superficially read books unfortunately, the book where he speaks of certain ghosts or spectres of Karl Marx (Derrida 1994), Derrida evokes a name—which is neither a fact nor a concept—to call this non-positive affirmation *justice*. It is the same name that Walter Benjamin evokes in many of his texts, understanding justice in his messianic manner and we know that Derrida calls this Benjaminian notion of justice 'messianic without messianism' (Ibid., p. 181).

There is thus not only more than one manner of affirmation, there is also more than one affirmation. There are affirmations, more than one, each one unique and singular, each one unconditional and unrepeatable, each one new and unheard and unuttered before. Consequently, there is more than one deconstruction, each arrival being absolutely irreducible and singular and each one is exceptional to assertion and negation. From this one thing follows: deconstruction does not have to be the possession of the person called Jacques Derrida, and that Derrida's singular gesture or style of deconstruction must not be the only deconstruction. Therefore Derrida rarely uses, at least in his early and middle career, the word "deconstruction", for it does not help us recognize a school of thought or a set of dogmas. At best, it is a signature of multiple, and each one singular affirmation—of the immeasurability of justice to law, the anachrony and asymmetry of justice in relation to law as such.

In his book on Marx and in close proximity to Benjamin and Lévinas whose names he does not fail to mention, Derrida evokes the idea of 'messianic without messianism'. It is justice which is this messianic idea par excellence. Derrida's singular gesture of deconstruction, then, amounts to an unconditional affirmation of justice. The idea of the messianic and this messianic idea of justice, thus, thought in a profound manner, is not at all an idea of a complete destruction and end to the world; it is rather that of an affirmation of a radical inauguration of the world, a waiting for a justice *to come* which is an incalculable and undecidable *coming* or *arriving*, the 'perhaps' of an arrival. What deconstruction, at least under the signature of Jacques Derrida, affirms is this justice that *perhaps* is *coming* or *arriving* (*l'avenir*), which—because it is incalculable and *perhaps*—is the idea or experience of the impossible as such. 'Wherever deconstruction is at stake', writes Derrida, 'it would be a matter of linking an affirmation, *if there is any*, to the experience of the impossible, which can only be a radical experience of the *perhaps*' (Ibid., 35). How can we understand this?

First of all, affirmation is in itself an impossible experience; it is an experience of the impossible. The radical affirmation, the unconditional justice, the incalculable arrival, the unthinkable other and the messianic violence is impossible to affirm. It is vertigo of thought, an abyss of knowledge, something like madness or death. Therefore it is still de-construction; it is the "de" of deconstruction—mark this negative marker "de". This "de", however, is not negation as opposed to assertion; it is not negativity as opposed to positivity of concept or fact. It is a radical, unconditional "de" of the impossible which is affirmation itself. The affirmation itself is impossible; otherwise it is not the radical, unconditional affirmation. Therefore there is no unitary "no" either. There is a radical impossibility of an affirmation which is other than negation and negativity; a non-negative impossible, if I may say that, tied to the affirmative itself. *One must affirm the impossible;* deconstruction must affirm the impossible: this is the ethics and politics of deconstruction. Or, better to put it in a manner that Derrida would perhaps like: wherever there is at stake the ethical and political, it would be a matter of affirming the impossible itself, which is the idea of justice, the 'messianic without messianism'. Justice is the experience of the impossible, not because it will never be realized, but because the moment of its realization is incalculable, radically heterogeneous to the order of law. Justice is irreducible to law, not merely because there is no law without justice but rather because if there is to be law at all, it can occur only in the name of justice and in order to realize justice. Therefore justice cannot be thought in terms of law. At each moment of the law's realization of itself, justice thus appears to be *not yet*, to be impossible, and yet *to arrive*. The time of justice is the time of "to arrive", an impossible time, which Derrida distinguishes from future that comes to presence in order to pass away. In the Biblical messianic conception it is thought as "remnant", a remainder, a still leftover when everything appears finished, the un-finishable after all finish, the un-endable after all the end, the never-ending arrival. For Derrida it is *justice* that is never finishable after all that is finished, the never-ending remnant. Justice is the end of law and end of politics and precisely thereby it is irreducible to the normative order of law, to the memorial order of history and to the pragmatic, calculable order of all politics. The "not yet" of justice, this immeasurable affirmation beyond all assertion and negation, radically interrupts the immanence of the normative order of law, opening thereby the pragmatic order of calculable politics to a justice always to come in an incalculable manner.

How do we understand this: to affirm the impossible? It seems, as it were, that the task of deconstruction demands that it must affirm the undeconstructable itself, which by an unconditional imperative must and should orient itself to the undeconstructibility—of what?—of the immeasurable justice, of the affirmation of the Yes, without knowledge and without concept. Deconstruction should, thus, not so much be concerned with the deconstructible only but rather with, first of all, the undeconstructable itself. *Deconstruction happens—supposedly this is the order of 'happening'—in the name of the undeconstructable; there is no deconstruction if it is not undeconstructable.* Justice is not thus subject to deconstruction, but all deconstruction—

of the economy of law, of the calculability of politics, of the conditioned nature of pragmatic—is carried out in the name of justice which is pure affirmation, unconditionally affirmed, but each time as radically new and each time as radically different.

## III

How do we understand this: affirmation of the impossible?

In one of his most beautiful texts, one that is very close to my heart, Jacques Derrida speaks of an unconditional forgiveness that demands to be affirmed each time without any given conditions, without any calculation by knowledge, without any mastery of the concept. Such is the enigma of forgiveness. A forgiveness that is forgivable, a forgivable forgiveness, the one that is prescriptible and prescripted by law and thus can enter into the economy of exchanges, into the circularity of conditioned and calculable negotiations and reconciliation, such forgivable forgiveness is, in the true sense of the term, is not true forgiveness. True, unconditional forgiveness must be that which is impossible to affirm and that which needs to be forgiven appears to be absolutely and unconditionally unforgivable. I don't truly forgive when it is already sought to be aimed at conditioned reconciliation and negotiations that will bring about the state of normalization. The order of law, which pardons only what is prescriptible by it, brings equivalences between punishing and forgiving. It, therefore, cannot forgive the unpunishable. But, since the unconditional and true forgiveness must forgive the unforgivable, it must thereby each time escape the circularity of law, the economy of equivalences of values and the exchangeability of forces. 'Forgiveness forgives', to say in Derrida's words, 'only the unforgivable...there is only forgiveness, if there is any, where there is the unforgivable. That is to say, forgiveness must announce itself as impossibility itself' (Derrida 2001; pp. 32-3). *One must forgive the unforgivable, otherwise it is not forgiveness*; one must affirm precisely the impossible, otherwise it is not truly affirmation, as if, as it were, one must thereby be signalled towards that which refuses any finality and any meaning, any intelligibility as such, 'a madness of the impossible' (Ibid., p. 45). Justice or forgiveness is an exception; it is a kind of eternity of an idea, which has an air of ahistoricity. To affirm justice demands that we affirm, each time singularly, the impossible and thereby risking knowledge or even one's self. It is an exception which is other than the other exception which is the exceptionality of the sovereign. The sovereign, who is an exception to the law and who provisionally escapes the circularity of law, has the possibility of pardoning the unpardonable, granting the mercy-plea of the accused. Derrida, however, when he speaks of the unconditional forgiveness, speaks of a messianic exception which for him is the true exception, and which is different from the exceptionality of the sovereign in respect to law. *A non-sovereign exception: such is the messianic affirmation of the impossible,* affirmation of a justice yet *to come*, of unconditional forgiveness without power and without sovereignty. Such is the order of *l'avenir,* of arrival: a messianic possibility or rather impossibility, without which there is neither politics nor ethics. Not that there should not be law and knowledge or politics, but rather precisely otherwise: true politics, in its very possibility, demands this pure, unconditional affirmation of justice. This is what Derrida calls 'democracy to come'. Politics, then, if it is to be possible in the true sense, must accept something 'that arrives which exceeds all institutions, all power, all juridico-political authority' (Ibid., p. 54). It must be able to say yes, and a yes and a yes once again.

# *Messianic Time and Deconstruction of Historical Reason*

This essay attempts to formulate a critique of historical reason from the perspective of a certain messianic understanding of time. Reading the work of Franz Rosenzweig, the German Jewish philosopher, we hope to show that Rosenzweig's messianic conception of time offers a radical deconstruction of the Occidental conception of historical reason as it finds its utmost fulfilment in Hegelian philosophy. What, then, messianic conception of time promises is that of radical interruption of the closure of history to open its violence to the arrival of justice that alone can redeem mankind. The time of language is thus not the time that commemorates and celebrates the sedimented and deposited memories of a given historical tradition in the name of a future goal to arrive at the end of a historical process; language rather waits for the radical interruption of the historical continuum that may occur at any time in an incalculable manner that brings justice to the world. It is only in the name of an arrival of such a radical justice that the concepts of "history", "memory" and "time", and consequently "politics" and "ethics" can for the first time become meaningful for us.

## I. History

A dominant conception of history—one that is philosophically grounded, in other words, metaphysically founded—understands history as an immanent plane of continuum, progressively and in an accumulative manner moving towards its goal that lies at the end of a process. Behind all that occurs as periodic breaks, it perceives a continuum of depository, sedimented values of which these periodic breaks are only the attenuated variations of that fundamental continuum. The philosopher, the metaphysician or the historian, then, looks back in a retrospective gaze to discover—beneath the variegated becoming of the historical tradition—the logic of movement that has fundamentally persisted in its self-same continuity through all these apparent discontinuities. The task of the historian or the philosopher is seen here to be commemorial. He is 'the owl of Minerva' taking its flight only in the dusk (Hegel 2008, p.16). The commemorial celebration of the historian and the metaphysician is celebration of victory of memory over forgetting; it is a feast of memory over that dreadful tyranny of time which brings dissolution to everything that arises in the world.

It is in Hegel's the philosophy of history that such a dominant conception of history finds its perfect commemorial expression. In the event of commemoration, which is the time of presence at the end of history, the historian then recounts the story of the triumphal march of the world-historical politics and how the progressive rationalization of reality finds embodiment in the world-historical institutions of earthly sovereignties. Hegelian dialectical philosophy of history is the most systematic Occidental theology (Christology) of history, a secularized theodicy of history (Löwith 1957). For Hegel, the figure of the Absolute, the Divine or the Spirit, must assume earthly embodiment on the immanent plane of world-historical becoming, as if, as it were God himself must sojourn on the domain of the worldly. This assumption of the embodiment of the divine on the worldly must pass through a process or a movement which is a series of sacrificial acts. The Divine itself needs to sacrifice itself and must undergo the suffering of finitude in order to be resurrected (one cannot miss here the Christological resonance). It is thus a movement of conquered finitude, of subsuming and taking possession of its own temporality of becoming unto itself or mastering of its time as its very own. The historical memory that commemorates is the celebration of triumph of memory over time; it is celebration of the power of spirit that has actualized the permanence, the endurance of eternity on the otherwise incessant arriving and passing away of the flow of time. The historical mankind realizes this eternity in the objective sphere of historical life in the form of political institutions, of which Hegel saw the modern State as the most perfect expression. Hegel's celebratory and commemorial understanding of history turns out to be the most monumentalized expression of Occidental reason in historical form.

Already Friedrich Nietzsche saw—and also Karl Max—within the same century when Hegel wrote those lines of celebration, the harmful, even destructive ideological underpinning of the Occidental, that is, of Hegelian theodicy of history, and envisaged, beyond the closure of such triumphal march of the world-historical politics, the possibility of a far more profound, a far more necessary and a creative forgetting, a creative "un-historical". That there is a forgetting far more profound than historical memory, a forgetting that is not a mere privation or a variation of memory: it is on the basis of such a possibility alone, so Nietzsche thought, that the world can at all be renewed and thus *freed* from the injustice of the world-history, can summon up justice and redemption to the world. Such an unhistorical history can alone be, for Nietzsche, the proper antidote to the world-conformist celebration of the "factual", of what already exists and what can be merely passed on to the ever coming generation in the form of historical knowledge (Nietzsche 1997a). Such deconstruction of the closures of history is renewed in the messianic critique of Walter Benjamin. For Benjamin, the messianic redemption, that is justice, cannot be thought on the immanent plane of the world-historical politics, for such a world-historical politics that progressively moves forward allows legitimizing of the past suffering of the vanquished and defeated in the name of a future goal of realization. As against such an ideology of victorious that assumes the form of historical reason, Benjamin evokes the messianic conception of history, a history that remains radically open to a future *to come* when all past suffering and injustice can be remedied, and that are not just trampled over in the name of an ever receding goal at the end of an irresistible forward march of the world-historical politics. Walter Benjamin's messianic conception of history is in close proximity with Franz Rosenzweig's messianic deconstruction of the violence of historical reason.

In his monumental *The Star of Redemption,* Franz Rosenzweig painstakingly analyses the very metaphysical foundation of the violence of the closure of historical reason represented by the Hegelian dialectical movement of the world-historical politics. Such violence adheres in the character of the "concept" itself that moves the Occidental discourse called "philosophy" from 'Ionia to Jena' (Rosenzweig 2005, p. 18), from Parmenides to Hegel. There is thus a "violence of the concept"—the concept, whose essential nature is to grasp and to master, to appropriate and to subsume the singulars unto totality, the differential and the multiplicity into identity. It is in Hegel's philosophical discourse of dialectical history such logic of subsumption appears in the most perfect historico-metaphysical form. Such subsumption in the economy of Hegelian discourse appears precisely at the moment when the waiting of mankind for justice in the radical event of arrival is sought to be included within the immanent closure of an auto-generative, secular version of a theodicy of history, and thus justice, instead of being the radical freedom from the violence of history, is seen to be equivalent to be the concept's self-actualization of itself.

At the heart of this process of the concept's self-actualization — which, for Hegel, is the name of "history"—lies the very metaphysical violence of the Occidental reason's attempt to master over the river of time that in the immense movement of its waves threaten to sweep away everything that arises and brings corruption to all that is generated. Hegel thus conceives history—and historical time—as opposed to the time that generates incessantly only to annihilate incessantly in a manner of sovereign indifference. This historical time, thus, is the possibility of preservation and endurance of works, thanks to memory, in the form of institutions of which the State is the most gigantic and valorised form. As historical beings, mankind is now *freed* from the tyranny of a time that incessantly generates and corrupts everything in pure indifference. History is, as it were, freedom *from* death itself by being able to make death itself *work* for the historical task of the historical being. Such a task is assumed by the State which, by the power of its violence that has in its disposal, arrests forcibly the free flowing river of life by installing dams, bringing discontinuities and halting stations to the incessant process of mere coming and going of life. The State is thus the power that makes possible the endurance of life in the form of law. The time of the State and the time of world-history is this time of law where continuity constantly renews itself through disruptions and discontinuities, flowing through dams and halting stations. Thus instead of the mere continuous time of indifference—of nature—there is now the historical time of law, which is the time of continuity through discontinuities (therefore a time of *differential continuity*) embodied in the State that renews the old law into new law. Since time cannot be stopped and the movement of life always triumphs, the only way the State must continuously insert life into law is by renewing the old law into new law. And this is, according to Rosenzweig, the metaphysical essence of all mythic violence that founds the State. In the following lines Rosenzweig points out the mythic violence that founds the laws of the State,

> This is the meaning of all violence, that it founds new law... Law is, as regards its essence old law. Now it shows itself as what violence is: the renewer of old law. In the violent act law continuously turns into new law. And the State is therefore equally as much lawful and violent, refuge of the old law and source of the new; in this double shape as refuge of the old and source of new the State places itself above the mere flowing off of the life of the people in which custom unceasingly and non-violently multiplies and law changes.

And again,

> To this natural allowing of the living moment to elapse...the State opposes its violent assertion of the moment...it masterfully seizes the moment, and every following moment, and forms it according to its will and its ability. At every moment the State violently settles the contradiction between preservation and renewal, old and new law. It is

> that continuous solution which the life course of the people constantly only postpones of its own accord through the flowing on of time; the State takes it in hand; in fact it is nothing other than this solving, resolved every moment, of the contradiction (Ibid., p. 353).

The time of world-history is this violent time, the time of violence. It manifests itself as power over time and an attempt of victory over death, not by annihilating it—for neither time nor death can be annihilated—but by subjugating it, by making it *work* for the possibility of world-history that continuously moves forward, through discontinuities, to its universal fulfilment. This violence that forcibly settles the contradiction between old and new, preservation and renewal is that very process of the State that constantly inserts the life of the singulars into the universal force of law, of the differential and multiplicities into the homogeneous order of totality. Historical memory that bears the power of the State and the dominant tradition is this struggle with the eternal movement of time and an exercise to preserve what seeks to refuse all preservation. In that process historical memory, through the institutional support of the State and family, solidifies its fidelity to what already "exists" by constantly renewing old law into new law, by mere extending what already "has-been" into today, hypostatizing the victorious past and allowing the suffering past, oppressed by the violence of history, to be forgotten in the name of a future goal of history. It thus legitimizes the past suffering in the name of the victory which will be realized at the end of a historical process, and which is celebrated in the commemorial tasks of the historical memory. The metaphysician of history, 'the owl of Minerva', who only looks back and not forward—and looks back only at the images of victory and not the vanquished—is the commemorator par excellence. He celebrates, monumentalizes the 'has-been' and forgets the radicality of the future which alone can bring justice (that lies beyond the law) to the unjustifiable, insufferable, irremissible past. The historical memory of the world-historical politics forecloses and represses what it presupposes: the other history, the history of forgetting, an un-historical history, the history of the unjustifiable, insufferable and irremissible. This other history does not celebrate the past that 'has been' but that condemns and passes judgment on it in the name of justice *to come* which has never been fulfilled on the immanent place of the theodicy of history and whose claims have remained undiminished till now.

## II. The Immemorial

Against such a theodicy of history whose unity is realized, thanks to the work of memory, in the objective sphere of spirit in the form of world-historical institutions like the State, Franz Rosenzweig evokes a messianic conception of an immemorial promise that, untouched by the violence of law, invisibly prepares for a universal justice and redemption to come. Being forever excess of the—and being prior to—memorial-commemorial works of law that are at the service of the world-historical politics, the idea of the immemorial opens us to a promise given to us before the law, which is the promise of redemption or justice. *This idea of justice is irreducible to law.* Emmanuel Lévinas' (2000) notion of the immemorial, which he thought in terms of *diachrony* (that is the idea of the non-co-incidence with any self-presence) of the future as the very event of the origin of time, is in a profound manner indebted to this Rosenzweigian messianic concept of the immemorial promise. Later Jean-Louis Chrétien makes this idea of the immemorial as the central concern of his works (2002).

Thus, Rosenzweig conceives a promise of justice or redemption given to us in an immemorial time which is in excess of all memory and which, therefore, does not occur *in* time, precisely because it is the event of the origin of time itself. At the origin of time—therefore it is before time, a time without time as it were—there lies promise, excess of all memory and therefore excess of all that can at all be commemorial. This promise is the promise of redemption. For Benjamin, this promise is the promise of justice for all those unjustifiable suffering of the vanquished and of the oppressed suffering in the triumphal march of the world-historical politics (Benjamin 2007, pp. 253-264). This promise is promised in this immemorial event of the world, which Rosenzweig calls "creation", that invisibly passes and renews itself through the event of "revelation" which is the renewal of the immemorially old, the immemorial ancient—the past before past, time before time—into ever new, ever presencing and the ever youthful. This movement of the renewal of the old promise into the ever new event of revelation, of the immemorial past into the ever presencing and ever youthful of love, is distinguished by Rosenzweig from the renewal of old law into new law by the State that, with the power of its violence, forcibly settles the contradiction of life and law, of preservation and renewal. There is thus another history of promise that moves towards its fulfilment in the event of redemption that does not coincide with the dialectical movement of the world-historical reason. There is another claim—the unconditional claim of redemption, the undiminished claim of justice—that is not coincident with the conditioned realization on the immanent plane of the world-historical reason in terms of the laws of the State. The immemorial opens us to the promise—which is not a specific promise but the promise *of* promise itself, it is promise *as such*— that extends time to infinity (Lévinas 2000), the promise before the time of the concept that violently subsumes the singularity into the homogeneous order of totality. The promise opens us to an immemorial justice before all violence. It is therefore an originary 'peace', an unconditional 'peace', before all war and before all conditioned peace. Not being completely realized on the immanent plane of the world-historical politics, because it is excess of law—and law is always violent—the promise carries in an invisible manner the character of "not yet". Justice has *not yet* occurred; redemption has *not yet* happened on the stage of history. Therefore there must come a time from a radical future, and that there must above all be such a radical event of future, a non-commemorial future, a future beyond the closure of history. This end(lessness) of time/history is not the time of dusk for the owl of Minerva to take its flight. For Rosenzweig, only a messianic time can inaugurate redemption or justice in the world in a future to come but whose promise must already have been given in an immemorial past before all past, in a beginning before beginning.

According to Rosenzweig such promise is already given in the event of language itself. Language is, therefore, not primarily conceptual, unlike what Hegel thought of language. At the origin of language, at the root of language lies there the promise; or, rather, promise itself is the root word of language, 'a speaking before speaking, the secret ground of speaking'. Rosenzweig goes on to say,

> Its original words are not real words, but promises of the real word. But yet the real word that "calls" the object by its name gets solid ground under its feet because the original word has promised it. What was mute becomes audible, the secret manifest, what was closed opens up, what which as thought has been complete inverts as word into a new beginning ... (Rosenzweig 2005, p. 119).

Time is thus opened up in this event of language as promise. It opens us to a time that is immemorially ancient and immemorially past on the one hand, and on the other hand, to an event of radical future of redemption beyond commemoration. Language is primarily this affirmation beyond all negativity. Nourished by the fecundity of this radically open time, language itself waits for redemption, for justice. It refuses to accept the historical tradition which merely transmits the already realized contents and values of the past through a continuum of memory and thus serves the sovereignties of the profane order. From Benjamin we know that such a valorisation of the immanence of historical continuum is merely an ideology of the victors. As against it the messianic time brings a radical rupture into the immanent field of historical continuum so as to conjure up the "not yet" of the incalculable justice to arrive today, for which we have always waited and for which time itself waits indefinitely.

### III. Time: Messianic and Historical

For 'redemption' to arrive, it must *not* be at the end of the scale of a very long time; it must not take a very long time where time grows quantitatively in an accumulative manner, step by step and in an infinite patience, approaching 'redemption' as it grows and ripens with the growth of world-historical politics that passes through the homogeneous scale of a historical continuum. The impatience of that demand for redemption must hope for it to come today, *hic et nunc.*

'Eternity, that is to say, must be hastened, it must always be capable of coming as early as "today"; only through it is it eternity. If there is no such force, no such prayer that hasten the coming of the Kingdom, then it does not come eternally, but—eternally does not come' (Ibid., p. 306). For eternity to come today, the immanent plane of the historical continuum who feeds itself upon the idea of progress needs to be deformalized and *interrupted.* Like Benjamin, Rosenzweig here deconstructs the positivistic, deterministic and quantitative idea of historical time that progressively marches to a determinable goal at the end of a historical process. The messianic conception of time, on the other hand, *interrupts* the continuum of the progressive march of the world-historical politics in such a manner that eternity which is future, instead of a very long time, may come even today: 'eternity is a future', writes Rosenzweig, ' which, without ceasing to be future, is nevertheless present. Eternity is a today that would be conscious of being more than today. And to say that the Kingdom is eternally coming means that its growth is no doubt necessary, but that rhythm of that growth is not definite, or, more exactly: that the growth does not have any relationship to time' (Ibid., p. 241).

Eternity which is *to come* from the extremity of future may, nevertheless, be present: this conjunction, this simultaneity of times is also the radical disjunction, the extreme non-simultaneity, the utmost interruption of time. The messianic arrival disrupts the dialectical movement and brings it to a halt: the clock time of the world-historical politics stops, but a new time begins, the messianic eternity, which is the calendar time of the liturgical. This beginning of new time at the extremity or at the end of time is already promised immemorially. This eternity that brings today together future and past, this eternity is not the eternity that is realized progressively, quantitatively, accumulatively. It is rather the eternity of the liturgical community that, in its singularity, withdraws from the participation with and assimilation into the false universality of the violent march of the world-historical politics. Instead of coercive and forceful seizing of the river of life by the power of the State, which is the time of the world-historical politics of the dominant Occidental reason,

Rosenzweig imagines the time *to come* for a messianic community that brings eternity in the river of life in the calendar of the liturgical. It thus does not need to be assimilated into the world-conquering and world-triumphalism of the Occidental history that progressively brings into its homogeneous order of totality all that is not Occidental (Greco-Roman); instead, through the very renewal of the immemorial promise of the past in ever new presencing, it can open to a time that remains beyond the destruction of violence wrought by both the violence of the incessant and indifferent coming and passing away of all powerful time, and the violence of forceful and coercive works of the historical time. Messianic time is thus to be distinguished from the horror of the time of the eternal, indifferential and mythic return of the same and from the violence of historical time embodied in the laws of earthly sovereignties.

## IV. The Other Singularity

The conception of the messianic justice, which is primarily a religious conception of the Jewish tradition, has certain proximity with the Indian conception of Avatara, a proximity that, however, must not be privileged at the cost of its singularity. As Franson Manjali (2009) suggests that the proximity or relation of these two singular conceptions may lie in the idea of divine suspension or interruption of the "profane" or "earthly" order of law, or even 'destruction of power', despite the fact that these two conceptions are based on two different conceptions of time. He then goes on to discuss at length Bhartrhari's (an Indian philosopher of the seventh century) philosophy of language—in its extremely complex relation to the problems of time and action—to suggest that Bhartrhari's conception of *Sadhu* who, through a melancholy internalization of all that has been past and of 'all the events of destruction wrought by time', can still 'look forward to a time to come with hope and promise' (Manjali 2009, p. 307), this conception has a certain proximity (of course distance) with the messianic affirmation of a time *to come* that involves an indefinite and incalculable bringing of interruption to the continuum of the order of 'political hegemony' (Ibid., p. 298) in the profane order. To make a complementary remark to it—a remark that is also made in a different gesture and in a different tonality—I would like to suggest that it is the singular gesture of the messianic withdrawal that Rosenzweig makes here from being assimilated into the false universality of a historical conception of the dominant Occidental political reason that has a resonance across a distance with the singularity of the Indian conception of Avatara or with Bhartrhari's philosophical conception of time and language. This singularity that resonates in the other, while maintaining its singularity, for me lies less in the similarity of discursive contents (philosophical or religious) between these two singular thinking but rather lies in this *gesture* of withdrawal itself, in this *very* movement of *hesitation*, in this *retreating* from the desire not to jump too quickly into the enthusiastic celebration of the progress of the universal world-historical politics, which we know, is justified by the dominant Occidental historical reason. This gesture consists of giving oneself time, to have time to receive, which demands an infinite patience that is a non-quantitative and non-accumulative, an infinite patience which is other than the patience of the concept. But this demands imagining of other politics and of other ethics *to come* that is neither satisfied with drawing inspiration from the already given past contents of a given tradition that are transmitted on the basis of historical continuum, nor such a politics is to be imagined on the basis of the ground of the factual that merely celebrates on what already "is" and therefore is capable of thinking neither the true "past" nor the true "future" of tradition. The gesture of inaugurating, or, at least, preparing for the inauguration of the other politics and ethics would rather demand that we conceive of the singularity of a historical tradition, inassimilable to the (false) universal and homogeneous order of the Occidental world-historical reason, in such a manner that it is exposed to the radical interruption of its very continuum. Such a singularity of a historical tradition does not need to remain closed off from the possibility of a true universality; it is rather that the radical singular mode of being demands that singularity is to be thought as nothing other than the opening of universality from the very heart of its being. To think such an ethics and politics is the very task of thinking in today's world.

# *The Labour in the Heart*[*]

Franz Rosenzweig in his *The Star of Redemption* understands the linguistic gesture of prayer in the Talmudic fashion: prayer as 'the labour in the heart'. It hints at the idea which Rosenzweig does not explicitly dwell on but implies in all senses of the word, the idea that the language of the labouring heart can be none other than prayer itself—the utmost and innermost manifestation of language *as* language without subordinating to the work of negation which the world-historical Spirit performs in its 'pathway of despair'. Linking this Rosenzweigian idea of prayer as the 'labour in the heart' to his larger philosophical task of thinking *linguistically* (*Sprachdenken* – 'speech-thinking', as Rosenzweig calls it), this essay attempts to make manifest the profound ethical gesture that Rosenzweig makes: that of opening to another "labour" and another notion of "the heart" than what the occidental metaphysics has been able to think. And what has thus remained unthinkable 'from Ionia to Jena' is nothing other than "prayer" itself, prayer that emerges from the very wound of finitude and thus clamours for redemption that cannot be fulfilled in the triumphant ethos of world-historical politics.

* This paper was presented at an international conference "Hebrew Language and Culture: Reception, Self-Conception and Intercultural Relation", held at Jawaharlal Nehru University, January 28-30, 2013.

# I

Prayer, so we hear the Talmudic saying, is the labour in the heart! What is it that ties up the labour—*in* the heart and *of* the heart—with this gesture that we call "prayer"? And, is it not surprising to hear 'the labour in the heart' and not of the hand, for is not it that labour so intimately and so profoundly bound up, since the Fall of man, with the destiny of his hands that has ever since marked him as what he "is"—that his "is" is "is not", a mortal being, inextricably mortal, irreducibly mortal? Thus, there seems to be a very profound connection between the mortality of man in his existentiality *as such*, and the destiny of his hands, destiny of his mortal existence that is woven with the destiny of his hands. In other words, the hands make the mortal a destinal being, better, the destinal being par excellence. This would mean that there would be no destiny for man if he were not given hands to labour. Should we make a reverse assertion: if he does not have hands, perhaps, he would not have such a destiny, destiny of mortality, of his mortality?

Between his hands and his heart there is more than one labour; as if existence, mortal it is, is nothing else other than this division, this separation of labours, and not merely that, it is at the same time their *belonging* together – hands and heart, each on its own labours and yet, each opening to the other, rendering the mortal as the labouring being. Not merely that, there are also his eyes – eyes that, in their glance, can look at the distance in the light that radiates from the extremity of space and yet arrives near him without leaping over the first nearest and without lingering at a halting place. The hands grope near about themselves and around in darkness; they are therefore tied up with the mortal whose hands they are, with his mortality, with the immanence of his condition, with the enclosure of his existence. Therefore man's pair of hands is the true expression of his destiny. On the other hand, the glance of the eyes welcome the distance to arrive at the nearness of the near in the light that radiates from an extremity of the source, invisible in itself, the light that illumines the whole path from the extremity of a distance to the nearest without any halting places, without leaping over the first neighbour for the sake of the second neighbour. The glance of the eyes thus *frees* the mortal from the destiny of his groping hands, destiny that he has to redeem from with the suffering of his own hands, destiny that falls into his hands as the inescapable condition of his existence, destiny encloses him with the iron cages of the law of the earth—the hands that must work with the soil and are bound up with the laws of the earth and with the march of world-history. On the other hand, the glance of the eyes, in the freedom and stillness of its look, welcomes the eternity to be the guest of today so that the farthest can be its neighbour without neglecting or leaping over the first neighbour. It is thereby an arrival without destiny, not as a privation of destiny, but because it is above or beyond destiny; it is, to say, with Franz Rosenzweig, "redemption" itself, for whose arrival the heart labours in its heart. Between the groping of the hands and the glance of the eyes that, in the stillness of its look, *frees* the mortal being from his destiny—what at stake, in this passage in-between, between the groping hands and glance of the eyes, is nothing other than prayer itself. It is here, in this passage, there moves the prayer of Franz Rosenzweig.

We are now at the very heart of Franz Rosenzweig's thinking of prayer. Allow me to make here one more step: that the question of prayer constitutes the heart of Rosenzweig's thinking as such; it is what moves his thinking but also his very existence at a very fundamental level where thinking or philosophy, if I can still use the word "philosophy", allows itself to be nourished by and in existence and nourishes existence in turn. If thinking is essentially linguistic—and this is for Rosenzweig what thinking is, in the true sense of the term—then existence of the mortal being itself is a linguistic mode of being: this is what Rosenzweig's conception of *Sprachdenken* or 'speech-thinking' would amount to, which would mean to say that the gesture of prayer, as the linguistic transformation of the mortal—between groping of his hands, and the glance of his eyes—must constitute the heart of language as such in such a manner and in such a way that in it language itself appears *as* language, where language manifests itself in its pure possibility, the pure possibility of language itself, the event of language itself. The whole struggle, the immense *polemos* or *agon* of Franz Rosenzweig with Hegelian metaphysics, and not only with him but with the 'brotherhood of philosophers from Ionia to Jena' (Rosenzweig 2005; p.18) lays precisely at this fundamental point: that what has remained unthought, what could never have been thought in Occidental metaphysics from 'Ionia to Jena' is nothing other than the gesture of prayer itself which is the linguistic transformation of existence, mortal from its very ground, demanding and crying for another exit from the iron cages of the laws of the earth, from the enclosure of its immanent totality—which philosophy has hitherto served, most successfully by Hegel at the pinnacle of the history of philosophy. At the last instance, Hegel's metaphysics has remained enclosed within the totality of groping movements— of hands, without being able to make any true exit, without being able to hasten eternity to arrive today and at this hour and without neglecting the nearest neighbour thereby. The claim of redemption, undiminished, despite more than two thousand years of Occidental metaphysics, therefore demands an exit, different from the exit that philosophy has never ceased to make in Plato as well as Hegel, an exit—from what?—from philosophy itself.

## II

This already says a lot though we have barely begun speaking. The fulfilment of the labour in the heart is radiated in the light from the extremity of distance, from an eternity "always to come", and yet that may, nevertheless, arrive near, nearer than the nearest, for the light travels space without thereby leaping over the near. What happens to language, then, with which the world becomes at first manifest, when the light of the messianic redemption radiates without leap and through this radiation invites the distance to the nearness to be its guest? Since I am going to read Rosenzweig with you and with your help now, I immediately supply here Rosenzweig's answer: language grows silent, like the deepening of time when eternity arrives, not because language sinks into nothing but precisely because in this light language fulfils itself completely. Like Benjamin later, Rosenzweig's *Sprachdenken* or 'speech-thinking' connects here the idea of messianic redemption with the event of language itself. *The event of language marks the messianic moment of redemption.* The appearance of the light to the glance of the eyes, and thus released from the groping of the hands, is the fulfilment of language *as* language, language as completion and not as mere negativity of the concept. 'It is', writes Rosenzweig, 'the silence of perfect understanding. Here, a glance says everything. Nothing teaches more clearly that the world is not yet redeemed than the multiplicity of languages. Between men who speak a common language, a glance very likely suffices to make themselves understood; just because they have a common language, they are relived of language" (Ibid; p. 313). But the glance that relieves language here, for Rosenzweig, is the deepening of language and therefore, precisely therefore, it is not a dialectical-conceptual movement of negation where language is forced to serve the empty gaze of the concept, where it assumes the force of law that is capable of founding the totality of universal history by denying the claims of redemption. Later Benjamin terms such false universal history of totality of the ideology of the victors as 'homogeneous empty time', in distinction to another universality that erupts as *nunc stans*, which Benjamin calls in linguistic terms and messianic sense the sober prose of citation.

Thus only as *nunc stans*—which is the glance of the eyes that releases us from the hands of language—the messianic can be the guest of language. From its very event of manifestation, language remains in its potentiality to welcome this guest of light, which is because language itself *as such* is this potentiality. The event of manifestation manifests nothing, reveals nothing new of language other than this—this potentiality of language to receive the guest of light to the glance of the eyes. When the light appears language itself stands still in the stillness of eternity. The light is the 'standing still', the *nunc stans* of language, not in the absence of time but precisely as its fulfilment. This light that blazes in the landscape of language arrives from the star which we, the mortal who speaks, wait for —

wait while speaking, while speaking we wait, for our speaking has a fundamental relation with waiting that opens for us the time of "not yet". In another text called *The New Thinking*, Rosenzweig makes clearer to us this fundamental relation of the event of temporality to waiting as the very origin of language as such. In speech time is given to us; or, we should say in a manner of Rosenzweigian spirit, language is the gift of time, is that which is nourished by time and by the possibility of a time that is to arrive. What arrives is the light from an extremity of the most distance, illuminating the nearest, bringing together the mortal and the world and the divine. The star of this light is the star of redemption. It is thus not for nothing that Franz Rosenzweig gives the title of the book as *The Star of Redemption*. Language fulfils itself in this light, and the heart that labours and has laboured from the beginning of its birth now grows quiet. The quietude of the light *frees* the speaking being, in the glance of the eyes from the hand of language by fulfilling it. This linguistic transformation that occurs here that frees the speaking being from the language of the hand is the gesture of liturgy, or the liturgical gesture itself.

Therefore Rosenzweig addresses the problem of prayer more in the third part, that is, the concluding part of his book than anywhere else. Liturgical gesture marks the event of the fulfilment of language. What is prayer if not the liturgical gesture par excellence: the gesture of the one at the threshold, anticipating the guest to arrive? Prayer frees the waiting being from the hands that grope around the near, frees him for the eyes that in the light sees the distance hastening near, "today" and "now", to this place and to this time. Is not what Rosenzweig calls "redemption" anything but this?—the hastening of eternity in "today", the joining of the divine and the mortal and the created together, like the joining of both the hands, like the joining of hands in prayer that joins those who are divided by languages—of stammering and of stumbling, but also of judgment and law and of the zealots and the sinners alike. To say in the spirit of Rosenzweig, prayer would then be nothing other than the gesture of joining the disjoined, gathering the separated that must pass through, must traverse through this passage between the hands and the eyes, between the multiple tongues and the possibility of one language, between waiting and arrival, between speech and silence, between time and eternity. But this liturgical universality of language in prayer, in contrast to the false universality of history as assumed by the ideology of the victors, must not be able to end in totality; the liturgical community must not end in the triumphal cry of the universal world-historical politics. Prayer, in the fundamental sense assumed in Rosenzweig's thinking, is rather an interruption of any totality, for where and when the joining of the hands ends in totality, prayer disappears too. To be able to make this gesture appear in his extraordinary life and in this extraordinary book and to make it available to us is the extraordinary merit and extraordinary importance of Franz Rosenzweig's *The Star of Redemption*. It is in this sense I would like to say today that the book called *The Star of Redemption* is written in the gesture of prayer which is the labour in the heart, the labour in *his* and everyone's heart, each heart beating and praying with the rhythm of that beat separately and each time together that welcomes the eternity "today", to the house of time.

Prayer, thus, in the spirit of Rosenzweigian thinking, is this *passage* of transformation, the transformation of speech from the hand to the glance of the eyes. This transformation is the joining of the hands that collect or gather language, or better, languages of the mortal in the deepening of a glance where the light of redemption radiates in the stillness of the *nunc stans*— distance touching the nearness and language becoming gesture, not the stammering gesture of multiplicity of languages, but the common gesture of prayer where singulars unite without being absorbed in one tyrannical and anonymous totality. In this manner prayer marks an event of community par excellence, or rather, we can say in a manner that will be more appropriate to the Rosenzweigian sense, that community, in a very essential sense, is essentially liturgical where liturgy of prayer interrupts each time the community becoming totality. Only in that sense, a singular gesture that touches the extremity of language, the gesture of prayer, that can at all evoke at the same time the possibility of universality beyond the particularity of "this" or "that" community, beyond "this" or "that" place, beyond "this" or "that" time—for the light of redemption must radiate on everyone, on each one, wherever one is and whoever one is, otherwise it is not redemption. But the universality of redemption does not sink its teeth on the works of the mortal beings who are, in a certain fundamental sense, are already "dead"; it does not profit from death of the singulars in the name of universality of the grand world-historical march of triumphal politics. Therefore it is necessary to make an exit, "another exit", one more and a different "exit". Prayer is the prayer of the one and of each one who makes this "exit", or, who demands an "exit" other than the exit that the philosophical brotherhood makes from 'Ionia to Jena'.

## III

Prayer is the event of language that passes from the groping of the hand to the glance of the eye. In so far as language is merely tied up with the groping of the hand, prayer does not happen to language and the glance is not illumined by the light. The nearness is either leaped over for the sake of second nearness, or one anticipates the arrival of the light from the distant star at the wrong time. In both cases, true prayer is missed, for the true prayer must be able to hasten the distant to arrive in the nearness of the near without leaping over the nearest near. Therefore the prayer of the groping hand that only fumbles over the near, and the prayer of the zealots that attempts to force Kingdom to come here and now—are false prayers. More dangerous than either of them is the prayer of the one whose destiny grows with the growth of the world destiny and that nourishes itself on the soil of the world-history, and therefore that always occurs at the right time and at the right place. Such prayers—the false prayer of the sinners and zealots and the prayer of the one always praying at the right time—are, for Rosenzweig, to be distinguished from the true prayer, the only prayer that is nourished in the light of the star of redemption. Other prayers, urgent though they are and are heard always, are prayers that are tied up with the groping of the hand and are never illumined by the light of the star. Therefore they often, willingly or unwillingly, march with the triumph of the grand world-historical politics and often sink their teeth in the soil of false redemption that totalizes without freeing mankind from the cages of the world, from the iron clutch of the law of the earth and from the languages of judgment. Only messianic languages can free the speaking mortal being from the cages of the law of world destiny and from the congealment of the river of life in the language of judgment. For Rosenzweig, and this is really my hypothesis here—which is barely hypothesis in fact—this messianic language, language fulfilling itself as language and therefore is relieved of language, this messianic language is nothing other than the liturgical gesture of prayer itself. In that sense prayer is the gesture of an "exit"—from the destiny of world-historical politics, from the triumphal *logos* of judgment that congeals life into law, from the *nomos* of the earth. It is prayer that frees life from law but, for that matter, it must acknowledge the groping of the mortal hand without totalizing the glance into the movement of the hand. Therefore, beginning with death, the book of *The Star of Redemption* has to end with life, with the inauguration of another life, life redeemed from the law of the world destiny—but passing through mortality, by passing through the bitter experience of being bitten by the 'poisonous sting' of death (Ibid; p. 9).

## IV

In his 1951-52 lectures delivered at the University of Freiburg entitled *What is Called Thinking*?, Martin Heidegger makes an astonishing remark: the mortal being called man who alone speaks, is distinguished from the other animals—and here Heidegger names especially "apes"—by having hands instead of merely having 'paws, claws or fangs' (Heidegger 2004; p. 16). Heidegger then immediately goes on to qualify this remark: the hands of man are not just to grasp—for even paws, claws or fangs can do that—but rather, and this is the most essential characteristic of hands, that they can join themselves together to welcome. The fundamental characteristic of hands is to welcome and to receive—of what?: the unthought, which is the most thought-provoking matter of thought, namely, the gift of thought itself, bound up with the gift of language which the mortal being called man alone can speak. Here Heidegger's deconstruction of metaphysics engages with the fundamental metaphysical determination of language itself. This occidental metaphysics of language determines language as language of the hand, hand that grasps, namely "concept". The German word for "concept"—and Hegel makes this word fundamental to his philosophy—is *Begriff* which comes from the verb *Greifen*, which means to grasp, to seize, to possess, to appropriate or master something. The immense movement that Heidegger undertakes here, via the mystics like Meister Eckhart, involves a "step back", a withdrawal, abandonment from the grasp of the concept, the *patience* of the concept as Hegel understands it. Hence is the profound importance of Meister Eckhart's idea of *Gelassenheit* for Heidegger, which is derived from the verb *Lassen*, which means to leave, to make an exit, to free from, to release something, but also to allow something to take place, to clear a space for something to occur. Now the hands, no longer the grasp of the concept, become a pair of joining hands. Thinking now, at the end of metaphysics, becomes "piety", withdrawn from the triumphalist *logos* of world-historical destiny.

For Heidegger, as for Rosenzweig, the hands are profoundly connected with the possibility of language for the mortal being. In another lecture, published as *On the Way to Language,* there comes another astonishing remark by Heidegger: the mortal being called man is given to language, as distinction from other beings, on the basis of a fundamental and unique relation that man has with mortality (Heidegger 1982, p. 107). That means, the event of language is profoundly intimated with mortality that first of all gives man his being and thereby *singularizing* each one and freeing the mortal from the grasp of the hands and delivers him to the joining of hands in the gesture of welcome. Between the grasping of hands and joining of hands there takes place the end of metaphysics and inauguration of another history, an epochal transformation of Being which Heidegger, as we know, calls *Ereignis*, the event itself.

In a serious sense, Rosenzweig—in his own words—is in an

agreement with the necessity of an "exit" here – from the grasp of the hand, from the *patience* of the concept. Therefore for Rosenzweig, language that is irreducible to 'the patience of the concept', this impatient language, is, in its impatience, groping of language rather than the grasping, seizing, mastering language of the concept. This impatience arises from the undeniable event of mortality itself but which must be denied in the philosophical language of the concept, impatience that *singularizes* each one of us and each one singularly, exposed to death and exposed to the necessity of making another exit. What is singularity if not that which cannot be included in the genus and absolved from the species? Yet this very singularity with its impatience of the groping hand—that language is—cannot be included within the philosophical system that conforms to the world-historical march of a triumphal destiny. The restlessness of the mortal cry that trembles in confronting the irreducible event of death constantly moves outside the *logos* of the world-historical politics, outside the language of judgment.

Hence is the necessity of another exit. This exit would involve freeing the hand itself, passing through its very joining that welcomes, to the glance of the eyes. Yet this gesture precisely, despite the radicality of Martin Heidegger's thought in proximity with the Rosenzweigian manner of thinking, could not be undertaken by Heidegger himself, even if the grasp of the hands is released open to welcome the epochal transformation of Being itself. But the hands themselves remain there unreleased; the piety of thinking has not yet reached the gesture of the other side of prayer, that is, glance of the eyes where alone language fulfils itself *as* language. What has thus remained unthought in Heidegger's 'piety of thinking', as it has remained unthought in occidental metaphysics, is none other than the gesture of prayer itself. Heidegger is one of the philosophers who came close to it when, for example, he thought the *Ereignis*, the event as without destiny—like prayer—and he too has experienced the stillness of silence in the blink of an eye. But there is between the blink and the glance of the eyes, there is little, very little, almost no difference that is yet so irreducible and so unthinkable even in the thought of the epochal transformation of Being.

# *On Beatitudes: A Critique of Historical Reason**

Can an unconditional happiness be based on the plane of the historical reason? If the task of the world-historical politics of the profane order is none other than happiness itself, this happiness is never the *conditio sine qua non*, since it is based on the relative conditions of the historical order whose becoming is marked by transiency and non-autarchy. Taking Kierkegaard and Plato as main reference points, I hope to argue that the singular notion of *beatitudo* is irreducible to historical reason and to any theodicy of history. Thought essentially, the demand of an unconditional happiness for the mortal being necessitates an eschatological opening of history to the true *conditio sine qua non*. Beatitude is the unconditional demand of the mortals that can only arrive as a gift that marks everything that is "human" with the wound of finitude. Nothing of the world-historical politics raises itself to the arrival of beatitudes, but only as the eschatological suspension of its law, and *abandonment* (in the sense of *Gelassenheit*, an idea from Meister Eckhart) of all sovereign claims, or all claims to sovereignty.

* I presented this paper at a national conference on "Singularities: Literature, Language, Philosophy", held at the School of Language, Literature and Culture Studies, Jawaharlal Nehru University on January 9-10, 2012.

## I

'Can eternal happiness be built upon the edifice of historical knowledge?' This question that we will ask today is the fundamental question of Johannes Climacus. For the time being, allow me to set aside the question of the enigmatic relationship between Johannes Climacus and Søren Kierkegaard. Could it have been otherwise than 'enigmatic'—this assuming of not just one but a series of pseudonyms, each meant to conceal and reveal at the same time that which can only be a paradox for us? Paradox, as we know, is a communication in the mode of indirection. The world and existence appear to us paradoxical when it touches the very edge of the world and reaches 'the extremity of existence', when all that familiar and harmonious, commensurate with our quotidian living away of our life suddenly appears questionable, strange and even monstrous. Does not all relationship when it touches 'the extremity of existence' (Kierkegaard 2009, p. 180) essentially become a paradox, in the sense that it must conceal in order to reveal, in order to incessantly name the nameless so that speech may not break off? It appears as if the relationship that one embarks at 'the extremity of existence' is like the voyage that one undertakes in a perilous sea from where one never returns without rendering oneself monstrous. Which eternal happiness does not know the essential 'peril of being' (Chrétien 2002, p. 22) where being must risk itself, essentially, only because to exist is to belong to this essential peril—'the peril of being'?

Can eternal happiness be based upon historical reason? First of all this question itself is paradoxical: it points towards, like an index, to what cannot be anticipated as meaning that is hermeneutically arrived within a given horizon of a "world", nor does it give us as a communicable content within a familiar context where the "world" is manifested already. Rather it presents itself to us as a riddle or as an essential secret that cannot be deciphered with an already known password. What is a paradox if not to see that is invisible to the eye and to hear that is inaudible to the ear? That eternal happiness may come to us today, *here and now*: does it not amount to seeing the invisible and hearing the inaudible—which we call by this beautiful and the marvellous word "promise"? That eternal happiness may come today, a "today" that is *not yet*, not yet visible to the eye and audible to the ear—such a thought of invisible and inaudible can only be thought on the basis of promise given beforehand, immemorially, *always already*. Paradox is the hinge that opens or closes existence at its extremity to an event of eternity that surprises us because it arrives contra all our anticipation, all our hopes, and all our expectations, an event nevertheless we never cease waiting for, for it alone promises us happiness, for it alone may make, if it were possible, our existence beatific and redeeming. What do we, then, wait for if not that which refuses all our waiting precisely because we cannot wait for it enough? What do we, then, hope for if not that which we cannot hope for it enough, for it never allows itself to be measured by the measurements of our hope? Such a "thing" called "beatitude" or "eternal happiness", were it to exist and were it to be possible for us, such a "thing" that we cannot hope because it is not given in our hope, such a "thing" alone *gives* us our hope, and such a hope for the unhoped-for would alone make our existence beatific and redeeming. What alone and what fundamentally makes our existence an *existence,* in an emphatic sense of the *verbal* and not in the nominative, is a paradox. We are that being that continually orients itself to that where no paths lead, where no passwords help. As a result, we are invited to do the impossible, in so far as we exist at all, to see the invisible and to hear the inaudible, to remember the immemorial and to anticipate the unanticipatable. This is what the Platonic idea of *anamnesis* is all about. Philosophy is fundamentally drafted on this paradox of existence, eliciting *astonishment* or *marvel* from us, enabling us to be surprised by the arrival of that which is even beyond "being". Whether we call it "Good" or by some other name, this "Good" alone is the object of our *astonishment.* The profound relation between the question of Good and the question of beatitudes lies here. They are like the two rays of the sun coming from the same source where the mortal cannot reach without being blinded, where one must learn to see the invisible and hear the inaudible.

## II

A paradox is always a hinge. The twisting and turning of the hinge is the moment of peril, whose sense is given in the sense of *metaphysics* as such, when one says 'Good *beyond* being'. The sense of peril is given in the transcendence that is constitutive of Good, not as an accident or a property of Good, but as an *esse* of Good *as such*. The Good is an excess of being which means 'to-put being at stake', or 'to put being in peril'. By putting being at stake, or by putting being in peril, the Good gives being its *essence*. The *essence* of being is after all nothing other than the Good itself. This means being can never arrive at its *essence* without putting at stake everything of itself. It must renounce its claim of immanence and self-sufficiency, its sovereignty and autochthony. Now this is the paradox: being is exposed to its *esse* at the very moment of its utter abandonment and highest mortification. *To arrive at its essence which is Good, being must first of all abandon itself.* Being must abandon its ground so that it may *come* to its essence, for the essence of being is this *coming* itself, in the infinitude of the verbal sense as an event and not in the substantial sense as "essence". To put at stake everything and everyone is to be *under* the immense question mark over the entirety of the visible realm of the historical, profane order. Everything and everyone must be abandoned, for it is the characteristic of the historical world that it is in "abandonment". The early messianic-eschatological Judaic-Christian theology of history calls such a characteristic mark of history as "apostasy" (*Abfall*). History belongs as predicate to the un-predicative freedom that groundlessly opens the whole world of the historical which as such in its entirety must pass away, since it is grounded in the ungroundable and inscrutable freedom. What is freedom if not that which is before any ground at all? (Taubes 2009, p. 5) Therefore the realm of the historical can never assume the decisiveness of judgment. Instead, it must itself be judged upon on the basis of a principle heterogeneous to it. The order of the historical must therefore be abandoned to its transiency, to its dying. Now this dying can never be an act of thought, nor be it the negation in the sense that Hegel grasped it as "concept" (*Begriff*). Instead it can only be related to the decision of existence.

In the works of philosophers such as Schelling and Kierkegaard who draw upon the messianic-eschatological tradition, decision constitutes decisive importance which they make an existential "category". Decision alone can be decisive. Only existence can be decisive and on that decisiveness there hangs upon the possibility or impossibility of an eternal happiness, not as an act of will or power of subjectivity, but as *abandonment,* in the sense we spoke above, of all subjective and objective claims to sovereignty. We know from Schelling what this idea of "decision" (*Entscheidung*) implies, an idea that Kierkegaard may have borrowed from his teacher: 'what-holds-apart-in-holding-together', the chasm of being. The German word that Schelling uses is more telling. The root verb here *Scheidung* with which the prefix *Ent-* is joined, implies divorce or separation, cleft or cision. All who have followed Schelling in this regard have borrowed this most fascinating and most beautiful word for this 'chasm of being', whether it is Kierkegaard, Heidegger or Rosenzweig. They call it *Existenz* in a very singular sense: not the identity of being and thought, an idea from Parmenides that has become the dominant task of Western philosophy, but that which *spaces* apart being from thought, rendering existence itself as excessive or ecstatic, unpresentable in thought. Jacob Böhme calls *Ungrund* that which groundlessly exposes existence to its ground that can never itself be grounded. Schelling, inspired by Böhme, names this unnameable as *Unvordenkliche*—what exists before the thinkability in the concept that sets the world apart from its foundation so that the world remains ecstatically open to its foundation without foundation.

Now *Existenz* is what-is-torn-apart-while-held-together. It marks the *mediation* (of Hegel's *Vermittlung*) or generation (of the Neo-Platonic 'emanation') between infinity and finitude, eternity and time, divinity and mortality impossible. An irreducible chasm separates them, while attracting them to the monstrosity of copulation. It is the Heraclitean agony of the *agon* that marks the *logos* of mortality, and Hölderlinian eccentricity that in its monstrosity holds together while tearing apart time and eternity, the mortal and the divine, melancholy and joy. Only in this monstrosity may there manifest beatitudes. The idea of beatitudes, or eternal happiness as Kierkegaard calls it, is thus essentially a demonic or monstrous idea; or it is rather an idea of monstrosity or demonic par excellence, for it is only on the basis of this monstrosity that the world of the historical may be redeemed. It is towards this point that I am attempting to move here, tying up so many diverse threads together. This monstrosity on the basis of which the whole transiency of the historical order can be offered an eternal happiness or beatitudes, Kierkegaard calls *Augenblick,* which is an excessive outburst of the moment when eternity arrives to us in the lightning flash of the advent. It is the moment when the whole historical order will arrive to its *essence* which is none other than its utter transiency. As Good manifests itself when being abandons itself, so *Augenblick* is the essence of manifestation because in it the whole realm of the historical abandons itself and thereby comes to its essence. In the abandonment of being, the Good *gives* itself to us as a gift which, as we will see soon, is none but the very gift of being itself.

To speak phenomenologically, the moment is the *donation* of phenomenality as such in the sense that it *gives* to existence its *possibility* at all, given as the fecundity of temporality. Only existence is a possibility, the possibility that at any moment of existence eternity may arrive there. That eternity may manifest itself today, wounding existence at the extremity of its decision, is a wager not guaranteed by finality or even a result of a calculated programme given in our knowledge. To *wage* is a putting at stake of everything at once without reserve and without finality, without hope and without anticipation, without projection and without protention for that, paradoxically, which alone opens up the event of the future for us. It is as if we must hope for that which does not allow itself to be hoped—the unhoped-for, which nevertheless may arrive from the extremity of future contra all calculations and all hopes. That eternity may arrive at each *hic et nunc*, that today there may erupt in the midst of my existence something like eternity for which I cannot wait, and yet which alone is worthy of waiting: this hope for the unhoped for is a deformalization of every series of numbers that I constitute, of every measurement that I permit myself with the time that is at my disposal and of every concept that philosophy permits me to attain. *If existence were only the hopeful for the hoped-for, then there will never be any wager, and eternity would never arrive to the mortal, and then existence, merely caught up in relative happiness bound to despair, like the relative regimes of earthly sovereignties destined for its transience, would never have beatitudes. Beatitude is possible only if the possibility is given to us to hope for what we cannot hope for—to hope for the unhoped* (Chrétien 2002). Beatitudes would then mean that which while wounding us with the irremissible mark of finitude, nevertheless opens us to the arrival of eternity that can never be hoped enough, and that must *always already* be hoped for, precisely because it is the only worthy of hope, the hope for the unhoped-for. Beatitude cannot be hoped for, for it is contradictory to all that can be hoped for. It is foreign to all that can be anticipated, programmed or projected by means of our power and of our capacity, of our law and justice, of our history and politics; and yet on the other hand, at the same time, beatitude is that alone constitutes, in the most eminent degree in any qualitative sense, what we must hope for and long for at any time when existence is granted to us, were such a thing possible for us, were such a thing granted to us. Since what is given to us in the eminent sense of an essential gift must first of all be *let-to* arrive, we can relate to such a gift only as renunciation or mortification of all claims to sovereignty, or all sovereign claims on the basis of the worldly power in the profane order. This is what Meister Eckhart calls *Gelazenheit* which Heidegger adopts in his own mode of thinking *Ereignis,* the event of appropriation. 'The event of appropriation' is paradoxical in the sense that *Ereignis* dispropriates us so that we belong to the event and not that the event belongs to us. *Gelassenheit* means *to let* appear that arrival without mastery, without triumphalism and without appropriation so that there may remain what can never be presented in our thought and which infinitely exceeds all our acts of grounding in the world. If what infinitely exceeds being is Good, then Good may not wholly belong to the domain of the nameability. If there remains the un-nameability in the gift and unthinkability in the

Good, then this reserve belongs to the essential character of the gift itself that while giving us abandons us, leaving us bereft of the ability to name it.

Thus nothing in the historical realm of self-legitimacy can attain beatitudes, because it may arrive only as an unconditional gift, since the gift introduces into the very being of our being an irreducible chasm, opening the foundation of our being to Good. The gift tears us apart from ourselves while giving us this gift of gift—being itself. The tearing is the characteristic of gift par excellence, thought radically. There is no gift without abyss, for all love is received with our mouth wide open, as the Greek word *Agape* implies. Now *Agape* not merely means love, it simultaneously means 'mouth opening wide', the hiatus or the chasm or abyss. What, then, love gives—while giving itself—is this opening wide of our mouth with which word flourishes, bursts forth, and nourishes itself. The early Christian theologians, even St. Paul in his *Letter to the Corinthians* uses the word *Agape* (which appears first in Homer's *Odysseus*) to name the Word of God which is Christ himself. In St. Paul, such an *Agape* is shown to be qualitatively different from *Eros.* What then the gift *gives*, before anything given, is this tearing itself. Our being must first of all be torn apart while holding us in this tear, exposing us to a fundamental cleft or separation. Only then may there arrive 'being', or better, *Existenz* itself. *Existenz* is in that sense a fundamental reception of the gift, the gift with which peril unceasingly calls us towards itself, as into the void. One could even say that what the gift gives is first of all this voiding itself. The gift voids away and makes everything new again; it transfigures us and redeems us by giving us the void, by making us *atopic*, without 'habitation and a name'. Beatitude is thus not of this world, the world that harmoniously coincides with itself or history that is contemporaneous with itself, for such a world is none but a *topia* that is marked by 'a habitation and a name'. *A-gape,* on the other hand, makes the world strange and *atopic.* It opens wide the mouth of the world, and sets afire the prisons of the world so that the migratory birds, the words, can fly again. The lightning flash of the *Augenblick* that sets fire to the prisons of the world is the moment of de-cision that alone makes existence an *Existenz,* an event of being. Far from being opposed to event, being would be none other than this event itself, the phosphorescence of an arrival whose radiance will show one day the paths that the migratory birds are to travel.

## III

> You have often heard me mention in many circumstances, namely, that something divine and supernatural (*daimonion*) happens to me—precisely the phenomenon that Meletus makes a joke of in the indictment. This sign, which comes as a kind of voice, first begun for me when I was a child; whenever it comes, it always forbids me to do whatever I am about to do, but never makes any positive commands."
> –Socrates (Plato 2000, p. 304).

> 'What then is Love?'? I asked. 'Is he mortal?' 'Of course not.' 'Well — then *what*?' 'As in the former instance, he is neither mortal nor immortal, but a mean between the two.' 'What is he, Diotima?' 'He is a *daimon*'.
> —Socrates (Ibid., p. 304).

There is always something demonic about the *eudaemons,* those angelic guardians that without our notice watch us, like expert night watchmen. The entirety of existence of Socrates is this *paideia*: a form of praxis as *asketes*, won through death, death being the most rigorous form of *asketes* or *aescesis*, as Socrates so movingly evokes in his *Phaedo*. Won through death, one thereby learns to *become* demonic. *Beatitudo* or happiness is essentially demonic. To become *demonic* or to learn to become *demonic* is the purpose of true philosophy. One must stake everything there; one must take 'the step of death'. This is the idea of Montaigne's "learning how to die" which is not a mastery of death, but an *aescesis* through which one learns to be abandoned by the world. The Socratic existence is this incessant, through daily *asketes*, attempt of this step, of this leap into the *demonic,* for the question of eternal happiness is the interest of *Existenz* itself. Undoubtedly for Johannes Climacus or for Søren Kierkegaard, apart from Christ only Socrates is the emblem or paradigm of the passion of the infinite par excellence. This paradigmatic consists of Socrates possessing unimitable and unrecognizable features and bearing strange or monstrous gestures to the point of ugliness. The singularity of Socrates for Kierkegaard lies in his continuous ability to maintain through the strangeness of his existence "the wound of the negative" (Kierkegaard 2009, p. 72), that "the thorn in the flesh" (Corinthians 12:7-10) without compromise, without giving way to aestheticism or to an ideal of familial beauty. Lacking "a local habitation and a name", the existential world of Socrates therefore appears to us as unfamiliar and incomprehensible. "Which have eyes, and see not; which have ears, and hear not" (Jeremiah 5.21).

The daimon of Socrates is the paradoxical existence. Being neither mortal nor divine, it *spaces* them apart by holding them together. The daimon thus marks the qualitative distinction between the divine and the mortal, between eternity and time, which being qualitative, is not amenable to the speculations of historical reason, to the calculation of the worldly powers of the profane order that can only be based upon approximation at best, at least when it is the question of eternal happiness. How can, then, eternal happiness be based upon the edifice of historical reason? Johannes Climacus' infinite interrogation is this infinite discernment of that which is a qualitative distinction and not a quantitative approximation; it is not a relative and attenuated variations of historical knowledge. All analogy between eternity and time that appeals to historical knowledge and to its pure positing power of law must be suspended here. Socrates' *daimon* never gives positive commands in the form of *thetic* but merely enables the suspension of law, for the true positive must be given beforehand in the very gift of being as sublime donation, before any opposition between positive and negative. *The demonic beatitude is the suspension of law, for it opens us to 'Good beyond the being'.* It is the renunciation of the analogy between the divine and the mortal, the analogy that is the source of all sovereign claims of the mortals. Instead the promise of beatitudes incessantly calls us to *Gelassenheit*—abandonment and 'to let be' so that *beatitudo* arrives in an unconditional arrival. 'To learn to die' in the Socratic sense is learning to abandon or suspend the work of law, and to contemplate through philosophical dialectic that 'Good beyond being' that arrives to us immemorially and which must be renewed each time anew in our life, unceasingly, as an infinite task of life. We must ceaselessly discover the Good in us that is given to us immemorially which is the idea of infinitude in us, through learning to be abandoned by the world, and learning to abandon the world of the world-historical politics.

## IV

Marked by the proper name, existence is singular, each time anew and each time—not yet finished, not yet completed. Ernst Bloch, in a Schellingian messianic manner, calls this "not yet" (*Noch Nicht*) as the fundamental character of existence itself. Singularity would not then be an accidental feature of existence as one property among others, but the very essential *how* of existence. *Existenz exists primordially and essentially as Noch Nicht.* Thus when Søren Kierkegaard writes "particular" as the *how* of existence, it is not meant "particular" in the recognizable sense of the term. First of all, it does not belong to the genus or species; it is not the beginning of a series of numbers; it does not belong to the grammatical domain of both articles definite and indefinite, as it slides away from all indications and each predicates. It is *singular* in the true sense of the term: it occurs only once, and once only. The thought of the singular is thus a tautological thought. Inserting it into the consolation of recollection of its eternal origin is a speculative compromise where *Existenz* is at once annulled. *Existenz* whose singularity is waged each time on the basis of its mortality is essentially and irreducibly finite. Now it is this mortality which is the indigestible remnant of the system, of each system, whatever name we give it, and under whatever denomination it appears. As Jacob Böhme speaks of nature—it is what is expelled or vomited out, as it is also from which one flees it for the sake of self-preservation in great anxiety, though it alone can consummate being and give being the possibility of its essence, that is, the Good itself. Such a "thing" called mortality appears to us only as suspension of law, for all concept, in the sense of *Begriff* (which means "grasping" or "seizing"), is positing, and all law is a self-positing immanence. Both Schelling and Kierkegaard's critiques of Hegel are fundamentally about this problem: how can the Good be thought on the basis of law?

Thus the universality of the world-historical progression, given in the concept of the concept itself, is the order of false universality. It posits only the visible order of the historical that must pass away, since it essentially is transient. The visible order of the historical cannot attain, on the basis of its self-consuming immanence, true universality, for it is marked by a non-autochthony and non-autarchy, by its non-sufficiency and by its incapacity to attain redemption by means of its own force. It can only be at best the realm of *apostasy*. One historical order passes away, giving way to another, often in the most violent manner, following the same law of sovereignty and same logic of legitimization. Even though one historical order is like a step in a ladder that leads you each time higher than the one before, still the distinction between these steps is a quantitative one. One thus never reaches the moment where eternity erupts "today" and "now", for time thought qualitatively, as Rosenzweig beautifully evokes in his *The Star of Redemption*, does not ripen like the fruits in the tree nor does it grow like steps of a ladder. The march of world-historical politics, as Hegel dramatizes in such an unforgettable manner in his *Phenomenology of Spirit*, is a march of history that ripens like a fruit, and when the whole of history makes the world like a wall, painted grey on grey, history itself becomes a museum of petrified images. The true universality, on the other hand, must speak in the name of an absolute that refuses the embodiment of an eternal happiness in any of its historical, relative, epochal manifestation, because it is based on the qualitative distinction between eternity and time, the divine and the mortal. Thus it does not permit in any epochal, historical order the embodiment of the divine in the human terms. Even if one historical order passes away giving way to the better regime, since the distinction between these historical orders is merely a quantitative one (Barth 1968), the world remains an *Agape* . It remains a chasm with its mouth wide open, a gap that does not allow the circle of history to reach the extremity of its origin and end at "one" instant, at "one" point. How can, then, existence which itself is this *Agape* find its eternal happiness in the order of the historical? Any attempt to bring this fundamental *Agape* to a closure will bring nothing worse than disaster. All theodicy of history attempts to realize on the basis of its power of law the divine on the immanent plane of history, thereby forgetting or closing off the *Agape* that first of all gives the world for us. In a very beautiful text, Jacob Taubes brings this point to a succinct summary: 'If the messianic idea in Judaism is not interiorized, it can turn 'the landscape of redemption' into a blazing apocalypse. If one is to enter irrevocably into history, it is imperative to beware of the illusion that redemption happens on the stage of history. For every attempt to bring about redemption on the level of history without a transfiguration of the messianic idea leads straight into abyss' (Taubes 2010, p. 9).

What is true universal other than the idea of redemption? The idea of redemption, which cannot be reduced either to the concept of an aesthetic totality or a world-historical system, is truly bound up with the event of beatitude. In the second theses of his *Philosophy of History*, Walter Benjamin evokes such an idea of happiness which is not the idea of happiness that human beings pursue in the profane order of the historical in the name of worldly powers. It rather arrives when there passes away what must pass away. We can say with Benjamin that the arrival of beatitude marks the suspension of law. In one of his early texts, Benjamin names the method of such a politics as "nihilism" (Benjamin 1986, p. 313). Such eschatological politics of world nihilism cannot be the aim or *telos* of the world-historical politics on the stage of history. Absolved from the mythic order of law that constitutes the tragic, it is even free from fate. Only then, fateless and free from the order of the determinate movement of the dialectical historical, redemption assumes the eternity of happiness. Being released from fate, the arrival of beatitudes is the true event, because all true events break out of fate, out of the immanence of destiny. This is actually, thought profoundly and in an unusual sense, what the Platonic idea of the "Good beyond being" evokes, an idea of Idea itself that is true universal in that it embodies itself only as singular and never as mere particular instantiation of genus or species. The singular is by definition an *Agape*. It is through the *Agape* that marks our finitude, existence is exposed to the universal which is not a homogeneous container filled with non-differential content but an incommensurable assemblage or constellation of singulars. Is it not what the Platonic notion of Idea is all about where the true universal is thought in relation to the singularity of ideas which are always finite in number and yet each overflowing to the Infinite, gaped wide open, like the mouth of the cave of the world through which the rays of the sun will one day arrive?

## V

Beatitude is the advent of the infinite in us. The possibility of such an arrival never ceases wounding us the moment the passion for beatitude takes birth in our soul. For this beatitude to be received, our existence itself must be an *Agape*, a tearing distance that enables nearness to be near us. *Agape* is nothing else but the birth of our soul; it is the structural opening of existence as such. Being marked by this irremissible wound, the mortals learn to partake the infinite, as gift and never as possession. The passion of philosophy or the idea of philosophy, as conceived by Socrates, is none other than this passion for beatitude. It is this passion that is the origin of philosophy, the passion that moves philosophy by touching the extremity of our existence. That there should be philosophy amidst the mortal human beings is not a fortuitous affair, as Heidegger keeps reminding us. It bears the infinite passion of Infinite, in an eminent sense, which is always to be understood existentially and not categorically. St. Augustine therefore makes beatitudes the highest task of existence, inseparable from the idea of being itself as a gift, coming from an infinite source forever inexhaustible in our naming of it and unfathomable in our thinking of it, because in order for that to be possible, the naming itself must *already* be a donation. For Spinoza, beatitude is attained by the highest mode of knowledge which, in distinction from all other kinds of knowledge, is love. It is not that knowledge which is the cognition of the world nor is it cognizing of God as he is present, but an 'intellectual love' of the One who is infinite in the most eminent sense. This 'intellectual love' is always attended by beatitudes, for we cannot love God other than 'under the form of eternity' (Spinoza 1955, p. 263). How can the form of eternity be loved other than as the love of life itself? Philosophy for Spinoza turns out to be the contemplation of life, precisely because it contemplates beatitude which is the true consummation of life, life as pure affirmation, not yet wounded by death. The word *Agape* in Greek implies simultaneously love and death, love that is ceaselessly in strife with death, and must be won through death, 'for love –as the saying goes—is strong as death'(Song of Solomon 8:6). 'A free man', writes Spinoza, 'thinks nothing less than of death; and his wisdom is a meditation not of death, but of life'(Spinoza 1955, p. 232). Johannes Climacus' question (Can the eternal happiness be based upon the historical?), on the other hand, is oriented towards an affirmation that must pass through *Agape*, for beatitude is an interest (which is *inter-esse:* in-between, a hiatus or gap) for that being alone who is irreducibly finite, and whose existence constantly presupposes the qualitative distinction between eternity and time, the divine and the mortal, the unconditional and the conditioned. As a result, she must continuously traverse the abyss, not as an immanent transition forming a continuum, but by a qualitative leap on the part of the being whose very being is a chasm and an essential peril. Likewise the order of history itself is nothing like an immanent generation but an order of finitude that must groundlessly be kept open, for it has groundlessly been opened in an immemorial origin that will never have any predicate in any historical remembrance. As a result the historical order, because of its non-autochthony and apostasy, must always appeal to an arrival heterogeneous to it for its consummation that must disrupt the whole order of the historical, in the name of beatitude that can never be realized in the profane order of the historical. The philosopher, then, must contemplate death, not in order to petrify existence and thinking with lifelessness, but precisely to seize and to be seized by that moment through which eternity traverses the entirety of our existence through the *agape* of death. Only then may eternity arrive today, and only then can the mortal attain blessedness, not on the basis of an aesthetization of totality, or on the basis of the tragic beauty of the world-historical atonement, but only on the basis of impossibility. This impossibility is a paradox that eternity may arrive precisely when all hopes for the hoped for have been finished and are abandoned. Beatitude is an eschatological idea, in the sense that it seeks its way out of any attempts at the world-historical totalization.

## VI

Can eternal happiness be based upon the edifice of the historical? Johannes Climacus' question of happiness is not at all the happiness of one self-absorbed, solipsistic consciousness shut within oneself and thus separating oneself from the universal. What Johannes Climacus is fundamentally concerned with is this promise of eternal happiness that is tied up with redemption that is true universal, and which therefore must continually put into question the false universality of world-historical politics. Thought negatively, Kierkegaard's eschatology is the critique of the world, and critique of religion itself, religion that institutionalizes in human terms (like any other human institutions like the State, etc) of what exceeds the power, the capacity or mastery of the "human", what can appear only on the basis of the paradox or a monstrosity, and what can arrive to us only in the unconditionality of the gift. Such a gift, while arriving to us, never ceases delivering us to the peril of our being. Existence is only *always already* singular, not in the sense of having a proper name shut within the interiority of inner consciousness, but rather precisely the opposite. For Kierkegaard, existence is the name of bursting out of immanence so that reception of the gift of beatitude may be possible. It is the spacing of an *Agape* which differentiates the one from oneself so that she can be given the gift of her being. Only such singularity which is the very mode of existence as such, the *how* of existence, can it fundamentally expose itself to true universality, beyond the universal logic of the historical reason. What Johannes Climacus calls "subjectivity" or "inwardness" is to be taken in the language of the parable in that it belongs to the 'indirect communication'. All profound relationships—like the relation to God for Climacus—that is taken at the 'extremity of existence' is essentially a parabolic or paradoxical relationship. *As life must be won through death, so eternity must be seized momentarily through the wound of time.* Beatitude is paradoxical: it welcomes the eternity in time which is never and never reached by the movement of the historical time of the world-historical politics. As decision is always taken at 'the extremity of existence', so the arrival of eternity happens at the extremity of time which is never to be thought as the end of a scale through progressive growing of time, but as an indeterminate eruption of something wholly heterogeneous at any moment of presence. Nothing is guaranteed here however. This is implied in the notion of faith which Søren Kierkegaard elaborates. What is faith if the object of faith is guaranteed by knowledge or by any calculable project and programme, to see what the eyes can see and to hear what the ears can hear? If beatitude is possible for the mortals, then it must be possible at *any* moment, and if such moment were to happen, it must break out of historical time of world-historical politics. Singularity is for Kierkegaard always this eschatological idea, an *Eschaton* that must be thought without finality and without end in the movement of the world-historical progression. The singularity of the existentiality of *Existenz* lies, in distinction from the pretension of a speculative thinker like Hegel, in that existence itself is considered to be eschatological in essence, in the sense that the possibility of its "any time" of eternity is such a possibility that even impossible must be possible. Beatitude is the partaking of the infinite, not as one possibility among other possibilities in the world, but as the possibility of an *atopic* that keeps the mouth of the world wide open. Never a capacity or a possession, beatitude is the reception of an unconditional gift through which the mortal partakes in the divine excess. But this reception demands that the mortals must renounce all forms of triumphalism and all egoistic claims to any form of sovereignty in the profane order. The excess of beatitude over each and every worldly claim to sovereignty on the basis of law, this excess also marks the very destitute character of us the mortal ones. More and more we learn to be destitute in the world, more and more we partake in an excess that comes to us as an unconditional gift, never as surety or as return profit of a judicious investment, but in an unconditional manner in the true sense of the term. It is a surprise.

# *The Infinite Contestation*[*]

The contestation-character of the relation between society and literature often comes to the question of whether, or in the name of what literature's (or, art's) claim for autonomy lies there the truly contestation character of literature, or rather it is in literature's "authentic", historical representation of society's suffering and oppression, so that literature can be seen to belong to the totality, or to the structure which is historical in character. In both ways, however, both "literature" (as a certain order of discourse, an institutionalized classification of certain texts, genre, etc) and "society" (its structural, its historical character of totality) are seen as given presences, and thus essentialized and hypostatized. What is attempted here is something entirely different: neither "literature" nor "society" can be seen as a given presence. The contestation character of literature lies, therefore, neither in its alleged autonomy, nor in its representational, "historical", character but precisely in its existential, unpredicative, non-essential and non-ontological character that infinitely contests any closure. Literature is neither thought here as a certain order of discourse, an institutionalized classification of certain texts, nor as a localizable part of an ontological totality and system, but precisely as an infinite movement of crossing, re-crossing, de-crossing of the line which cannot be ontologized, and therefore can never be completely

---

* This paper was read at a conference on "Society and Literature", organized by ICSSR and North East Hill University, Shillong, March 16-18, 2010.

> assimilated to any closure without remainder. It is this remainder which is called "literature", a remainder which is the very condition of literature's opening of the world, and its messianic manifestation of the society to come. This essay reads the works of Heidegger, Blanchot, Benjamin and German Romantics to raise the old question again, but in a new way, to think the infinity of literature's contestation to any closure, including its own closure and its messianic, utopian affirmation of a society yet to come.

## I

We are concerned here with the relation between literature and society. We shall see that this strange relation is essentially the question of contestation, nor of *this* or *that* contestation but a contestation infinite and unconditional. We shall see that this question of contestation is above all the question of *limit*, not just the dialectical limit between two concepts with its sublation (*Aufhebung*) into the third, but an infinite limit that calls upon itself its own erasure in its very movement of contestation itself, without resolution, without *Aufhebung*.

## II

Today a major portion of theoretical questions in literary-philosophical studies of our academic institutions are concerned with the limit-question of philosophy-literature and aesthetic-political, bringing along with it the question of "limit" again. What has come to be known as *deconstruction* raises nothing but this question of the *limit* itself anew—of the closure of certain metaphysics, of ontology and logic, of what has predominantly come to be known as *philosophy*. With this question, contestation of deconstruction attempts to open up the closure of philosophy to the unconditional, messianic affirmation of future, the infinite yet *to* come. This infinite contestation, in so far as it is *infinite*, always carries an often incommensurable, aporetic double gesture: a negative (but not dialectical) and an affirmative (but not positing): an infinite interruption and voiding of what is already given, unworking the sedimented, essentialized artifice and at the same time affirming an unconditional future, an unconditional ethics of the other *to* come.

It is this *in-finite* character of contestation that is the matter of thinking today, contestation that contests not only of what is given, any *this* or *that*, but of any notion of Being and ground as such. The infinite contestation is the infinite movement of contestation without positing foundation and ground of this very contestation, of which we can thus say that the infinite contestation is contestation *unconditional*. In its infinite movement of contestation, it erases its own ground and its Being, so that the Being and ground of contestation can only be its own erasure. It is this erasure that is the task of thinking today in its very un-thinkable abyss that calls upon thinking to its highest exertion.

What is thus at stake with the question of limit is not the dialectical limit between two concepts, but the infinite limit between the conditioned and the finite and the unconditioned as such, a limit which is without possessing resolution of a sublation (*Aufhebung*). If literature is the question of limit, but not of relation, nor of values between philosophy and literature, then this strange name 'literature' can neither be reduced to a certain order of discourse, nor to an institutionalized classification of certain texts, genres, etc., but more essentially as *an infinite contestation* that in *voiding away* of the sedimented given, affirms what is *not yet* as an unconditional affirmation of the future to arrive. It is in relation to the question of contestation, understood in the verbal resonance of its infinitive and understood in its double gesture, that we shall raise here again the question of the relation between literature and society.

As one can see that hereby the traditional debate between the two notions about the relation between literature and society is displaced, the debate that concerns itself on the one hand with literature's claims to autonomy and thereby its bitter refusal, rebellion or insubordination to serve the Universal which society imposes upon it, which is in fact nothing other than a partisan, parochial, ideological claim to totality; and on the other hand, the debate concerns itself with claims of the society's universal that imposes upon literature a normative task, that of representing society's injustices and sufferings, helping society to accomplish its *telos,* which is that of its absence of suffering. This normative task is inseparable from a certain ontological-aesthetic paradigm, a paradigm that brings together the ontology of the social with the aesthetic, determining literature and art as essentially mimetic and representational: art as *figuration* of the socio-political, or socio-political as *figuration* of the aesthetic. From here we can go further, that the traditional metaphysics from Plato to Hegel, in so far it is an *onto-logy* as such, is none other than an ontology of *figuration*. At stake here is an immense task which is that deconstruction of the *onto-figuro-logy* must accompany a loosening the sedimented structure of the metaphysics of the political, opening to the entirely new understanding of what we mean by 'politics' and 'society', no longer on the basis of the *figuration* of Being. Some fascinating works, especially that of Philippe Lacoue-Labarthe (1998) are devoted to this question.

The relation between literature and society, then, has to be addressed outside the above mentioned debate, outside the *onto-figuro-logy*, outside the determination of art as figuration of the socio-political, or socio-political as figuration of the aesthetic. Displacing this debate, this reductive notion of contestation will be sought here to be opened up to an infinite contestation that brings into play at the same time the aporetic double gesture mentioned above, thereby putting into question the ontological presupposition in the aesthetic *figuration* of the social and socio-political *figuration* of the aesthetics, so that the very notions of 'literature' and 'social' themselves are no longer thought of in their given determinations but are opened up to their event-character, to their open character to the unconditional future, to the *not yet*, outside the figuration-logic of Being. Literature, even before an order of discourse, or a certain institutionalized classification of certain texts according to genres etc, is rather an opening of the world, a manifestation of the coming, and as such is *social* before any society that is sedimented, essentialized and figured on the basis of "ground" or "subjectivity". If this is so, then the *event-character* of literature can no longer be understood on the basis of the figuration logic of Being, but as infinite movement of contestation which, as contestation, is the movement of ruination or *disfiguration* and at the same affirming the *not yet*. But this is only in so far as the infinity of this negative movement does not allow itself to be assimilated into any totality, or system without remainder.

What, thus, remains outside totality or system, outside any ontological ground of positing, outside any metaphysics of subjectivity, is nothing but the *social*, not in the sense of *this* society or *that* particular society that has been given to us (which can be predicated and predicted, a conditional and conditioned society), but rather in an unconditional sense of *social* such as *promise* which is always to arrive, the *social* that is not yet, the social that will never yet figure itself on the basis of the logic of Being. Understanding in this messianic sense, I would venture to say that *literature is precisely the movement of the social, or better, is the promise of the social,* since in its infinite movement to the outside the given presences, welcomes the others who do not belong to any given society, to any world, to any normative juridical-legislative totality. This is so only in so far as literature itself is without any society of its own, since its infinite movement character of contestation erases its own ground of positing, and thereby affirming *the social* unconditionally without aesthetizing and essentializing it. Such a social must bear the promise of the unconditional in its movement, and in its *event-character*, which is that of welcoming the others who do not have society of their own, the society-less, the homeless, the exiled and the excluded, the pre-inscribed and pre-signified others. *Literature is social*, neither because literature is in its innermost ground representational of the *given* mode of being of a society, nor so much because literature as representational is primarily inscription of the monumental, the victorious, but it is rather otherwise: literature, since it infinitely voids away any metaphysics of subjectivity or ontology, egology or phenomenology of consciousness, inserts this very void in the heart of any given mode of being of a society, or of the world. The logic of the world, or of society, or even of the political cannot be separated from the world's irreducible abyss in its very heart, for it is only on the basis of this void (this infinite nothingness that cannot be dialectically sublated into the speculative unity of the Universal)—which is not a basis at all, neither being nor ground, neither substance nor essence—that there arrives the others in place of "I". Writing, or better literature is essentially social, not so much because it faithfully represents as mimetic signification the fullness of the community's or society's self-presence, but rather because literature introduces an incompletion, a void, nothingness, an 'irreducible remainder' (Schelling 1936, p. 34) in the very heart of community, and thereby opens the closure of society to those who are outside in an unconditional welcoming and hospitality (Derrida & Doufourmantelle 2000).

Literature therefore, is not so much the triumphal march of the so-called 'speech-community' but the melancholic cadences of the society that opens the heart of society or community to its *atopia,* to its outside which is not yet a place, a habitation, or dwelling. Only such an *atopia* can constitute the utopia for society, its messianic hope for the *Not Yet.* Literature, beyond and outside its topical character, introduces at the heart of a dwelling of the society, something like an *atopic, a transcendence of the arrival, outside the closure of any immanence of self-presence.* Hence there always lies something non-historical, non-temporal (rather than a-historical and a-temporal) of literature, an *already-always* character, of an immemorial past of a promise that has not yet gathered itself into the unity of a dwelling, an 'irreducible remainder' of any given mode of being of a society, an eternal remnant of any given presence of a society, rendering each society like an open, exposed wound, a sundered, dismembered opening to the not yet.

Literature is society's eternal remnant.

## III

When one says that literature is society's eternal, messianic remnant, we say almost nothing concerning literature in its "what-content". Is not the question: what *is* literature?: the metaphysical question par excellence, like the question: *what is Being*? If literature is the *limit* of philosophy, heterogeneous, excess, the outside of philosophy, then we may not any more ask the question of literature as: 'what *is* literature?'. Is it not the philosophical question par excellence, like the sublime philosophical question: 'what is Being?' Thus Martin

Heidegger recalls that the question 'what is Being?', as in the traditional metaphysical discourse, already tacitly presupposes Being as 'given presence' (Heidegger 1962), beings *already* there as entities existent. In other words, the question of Being is asked in the traditional metaphysical discourse—Being in its what-character and being in so far that *is*—as the question of beings as a whole, in its totality. The exhaustion of this metaphysics, its fatigue and unworking of itself lies in that the question of Being can no longer be asked in terms of the question of beings as a whole —therefore not as: 'what is Being?'—but as the very question of *difference*, as a differing of questioning, *of the erasure of Being;* not: Being as 'given presence', but *coming to presence* of Being, Being in its event-character, Being in its futural non-closure outside any reductive metaphysical totalization. This signifies that the question of Being has become undecidable, the *line* that demarcates Being from Nothing itself has become no longer a localizable limit; it has become *a-topic, without dwelling and without name*. If the line enables us to make decision and therefore is the condition of possibility of a judgment, whether assertive or not (that something *is* which in turn presupposes the given-ness of a being *about* which a judgment is made and predicated); the undecidability of the line would imply that the judgment concerning the being itself has become undecidable. The sovereignty of logic as the measure of our thinkability has given way to the vertigo of the unthinkable.

## IV

The relationship between the line, or the limit and decision as it functions in the metaphysical understanding of Judgment is complex. Hegel understands the limit as determinate negation. The limit, in its negativity, enables a being to be what it is, *that it is so* and not otherwise. Thus Hegel writes, 'In Being-there-and-then, the negation is still directly one with the Being, and this negation is what we call a Limit (Boundary). A thing is what it is, only in and by reason of its limit. We cannot therefore regard the limit as only external to being which is then and there. It rather goes through and through the whole of such existence' (Hegel 1975, p. 136). In other words, limit is always determinate of a being in its negativity. It alone enables judgment that a being is *so*, because of its difference from the others, because it limits and is limited by others. The decision concerning beings arises, in Hegelian philosophy, as a determinate action: decision negates that from which it emerges; it negates its origin and differs from this origin to be what it is. Thus the question of decision—as determinate negation, or through setting up the line, the limit—is inseparable from the question of difference or discontinuity. But difference, in so far as it cannot maintain itself (it does not yet have a being of its own), must re-turn to the origin, to the Same, through this very negation, once more, of this line, of this limit, of this finitude. This is how the question of the line functions in Hegelian philosophical discourse: the line is always only transitive; it separates and through separation con-joins, gathers into the unity of a ground. This conjunction is judgment, Hegelian speculative judgment. Since the judgment *arrives* itself, *comes* to itself, not only negating any immediate indeterminate, but also the finitude of the mediated determination, Hegelian notion of judgment is the *speculative* judgment (Hegel 1998). The infinite-speculative judgment, experiencing finitude (that of the process, of coming and arriving), can be arrived only as result, as the accomplishment result of the dialectical process of mediation. It is precisely because of this Hegelian speculative, infinite judgment remains *predicative*, a sort of re-membering, or re-counting of what must already have *been*.

This is the secret connection between the traditional Ontology, coming down from Aristotle, with Logic: the predicative proposition, whose sovereignty even Hegel did not question radically, presupposes Being as "given presence", that asks: 'what is Being?' with a reply: 'S is P'. The difference between Logic and Ontology as two separate areas of questioning in philosophy departments of our universities is only derivative; they already presuppose the more originary connection between the question of Being and the question of judgment. Therefore a questioning of this questioning must at once reveal the forgotten, concealed connection between the two. A critique of the traditional ontological questioning of Being (as 'given presence') is at once a critique of the traditional logical determination of judgment (a predicative proposition). The question of Being that is *not* "given presence" can thus not to be questioned as in predicative judgment (as in: 'what is Being?'), since the question of Being is already forgotten, already withdrawn, already erased when the question of Being is asked in the manner: 'what is Being?'. Here philosophical thinking comes to its aporia: the necessity and yet the impossibility of thinking, not of Being that there is, that can be predicated, that can be asked in 'what is?', but the very erasure of it, which will already always be erased, in the future of a past.

## V

What happens when the line always transgresses and is transgressed in a manner that transgression does not maintain itself, when it erases itself? Does not thereby the line, refusing to arrive at a determinate predicative judgment *about* what already has *been*, rather opens itself towards the undecidable, un-predictable coming of a *not yet*, so that instead of con-joining between what has been and not yet, it creates the void *between* the two? The abyss of the limit or the infinite contestation of the line therefore always carries incommensurable, aporetic double moments. By rendering judgment undecidable and instable, by interrupting the sedimented, substantialized, essentialized closure of any reductive totalization, it silently prepares for a "yes" for the "not yet", enabling us confront the abyssal ground of judgment itself. Is it not nihilism par excellence: the copula as the void, as interruption?

As we can see that it is Nietzsche's question par excellence, for it is he who more than anyone else has made us aware that the question of the line is essentially a question of Nihilism. The line is the limit where all values devalue themselves and yet this line is also that which devaluing all values, prepares us for the transfiguration of these values themselves. Only in confrontation with nihilism can an essential transfiguration of nihilism be accomplished. This is truly the messianic, affirmative, *Yes* saying moment in Nietzschean discourse.

Therefore Heidegger's (1998) thinking on the question of the line, in his response to Ernst Jünger, is at once thinking on nihilism, not of asserting the necessity of nihilism, but to enter into the confrontation with the essence of nihilism in an essential manner so that a thought of the future beyond nihilism may be affirmed.

The experience of the political and social, where neither "political" is understood in the legislative-juridical manner, nor "society" being understood in the dialectical-speculative manner but rather as a messianic affirmation of the 'not yet', this experience of the political and social will, then, be the very experience of the interruption and contestation. Thus entering into confrontation with the void is for us now, more than ever before, the very task of the political, the task of interrupting, the task of inserting the line of the undecidable between what has already been and the not yet. This task of the political demands that the notion of judgment be thought anew: *cision* into the very heart of *de-cision* and judgment, a discontinuity into the transition from what has been to not yet be introduced so that what remains of the innermost unity of ground (as condition of the possibility of judgment) remains an *Ungrund*.

With the undecidability of the line, not only the *positing* of an immanent totality and its ontological ground, but also the *positing* of transcendence with its ontological ground too is interrupted. What remains, without remaining anything, is this ontological void, a non-positing and non-negative affirmation of interruption. Schelling (2000) calls it *Abgrund:* abyss that incessantly interrupts and contests infinitely whatever seeks to be grounded as totality.

## VI

Schelling's deconstruction of the dominant metaphysics of judgment is extremely complex. What Schelling calls *Abgrund*, the unconditional ground of existence, can never be sublated into the logic of Being and it cannot be made to serve the predicative function of logical truth. Instead, the abyss of the ground (which is neither being nor pure nothing, but an excess, the heterogeneous, the outside) remains outside the conditioned existence as something like an 'irreducible remainder' (Schelling 1936, p. 34). Thus there always remains in finite existence something like its outside which it cannot recuperate, its ground that remains groundless, its past that has never been presence and will never present itself, something of a kind of self-un-accomplishment, a movement without work, incompletion that never attains complete being, a void that haunts us with its eternal veil of melancholy.

Here Schelling's distinction between existence and its ground is thought in relation to the line—the copula of the judgment—that separates each from other, and in this separating, gives itself to the other; each is drawn towards the other in this drawing away, in withdrawal from the other. As a result, this caesural, abyssal (non) relation between ground *and* existence can never accomplish the innermost unity of the logical truth. The line interminably, unceasingly introduces an irreducible interval, an unthinkable hiatus, vertigo of the abyss between subject and predicate, ground and existence. Therefore the line itself can no longer be ontologically thought as *given being*, for to think the line, the line itself must *give* this very thinking. Schelling therefore paradoxically calls this, while referring to God's decision to reveal himself, as 'un-pre-thinkable' (Schelling 2000). Thus even God needs an un-pre-thinkable ontological void, an affirmation and opening of an outside of himself, a *freeing* for the coming. It is here Schelling sees the abyssal source of human freedom, born out of an 'un-pre-thinkable' (*Unvordenkliche*) de-*cision* (*Entscheidung*), the unconditional source that lies outside the line, forever non-appropriable, for the source itself is not posited by man himself, but granted to man as pure, unconditional *offering* of which Schelling (Schelling 1936, p. 79) speaks as "loan". The line is 'un-pre-thinkable' because it itself gives and comes to thinking, to the presence of thinking and to the thinking of presence. The line that enables decision to emerge and enables judgment and predication, itself thereby always—without positing itself as excess—exceeds decision. De-cision is nothing other than the cision, the cut that separates something as non-appropriable outside of what comes to be decision at all.

Therefore *there cannot be predication about the line*, for the line alone enables predications and judgment, interminably thereby exposing itself to its limit. The line has the relation to the *always already* past (*Gewesenheit*), to what has *immemorially* fallen (*Abfall*) outside existence, outside predication and judgment, outside decision and being. Therefore the distinction between ground and existence cannot be dialectical opposition at the service of a speculative unity. It is rather a relation of a non-dialectical difference with the abyss where unity remains unattained, unaccomplished, un-done. It does not enable (or rather it continuously contests and interrupts) the project of positing the outside as the heterogeneous, as ontologically grounded transcendental point from which to contest any discourse of immanence. Rather the line itself happens as *infinite contestation*, contesting not only "this", but also "that". It contests its own contestation interminably and infinitely. The infinite contestation not only contests "this" or "that", but also the very ground of contestation. It un-grounds itself in the very grounding of what comes to presence, what comes to be, rather than lying somewhere as inert, independent, posited transcendental ground.

The question is no longer, as Schelling himself thought in his early years, of thinking art and literature as *synthesis* of unconscious and conscious, as 'unconscious production' (Schelling 1993) of the works of an artistic genius, but rather now it is the question of a disjunction, a dehiscence of the line that is the abyss. The great idealist project of the philosophical discourse of Absolute, which Schelling himself dreamed of in his early years, ends here. No longer being able to found itself, ground itself as outside, as excess, literature disappears, infinitely and interminably. It interrupts and contests infinitely whatever seeks to be grounded as Absolute, including itself. It contests itself thereby, itself disappearing (Blanchot 1993, pp. 351-9), a dying beyond negation.

## VII

Out of this essential experience of the line the question of poetry or literature becomes a question to philosophy whereby literature comes to contest itself infinitely, to interrupt itself and to call itself into question. Literature that has become a question, to philosophy and to itself, thereby not only contests the philosophical 'question' and the philosophical manner of questioning, it also thereby questions its very manner of questioning from certain ground as 'literature' outside 'philosophy'. Such is the *infinite question* of literature, the infinite question *to* literature, the questioning of the question; it is the question of literature's erasure, its withdrawal, and its non-possibility.

When the line becomes undecidable—between poetry and prose, between literature and philosophy—then literature, threatening to be everything in a sovereign manner and unfolding to the absolute becoming, disappears without end, as if the sovereignty of literature is inseparable from its disappearance, its destruction, its self-abnegation. Who more than Maurice Blanchot has brought to our vigilance the strange phenomena, or movement called "literature" that disappears in its very apparition, for its essence is to be without essence: that of ruination and worklessness beyond *telos*, interminable, unceasing movement of negation? Out of the experience of this question, which henceforth will be experienced as that of interruption, the place of literature has come to occupy in the German Romantic's thinking of literary work and the task of criticism. This is what determines the famous quarrel between the ancients and Romantics. Literature is no longer determined to be an experience of the foundation without thereby its simultaneous interruption. This has profound ethico-political significance for us, as the early German Romantics themselves were aware of. Already, in proximity to and distantiating from Fichte's notion of *Positing*—thus instead of positing "I" in opposition to Non-I in a Fichtean manner—a notion of *reflection* is developed in early German Romantics which cannot be reduced to the predicative proposition. Since the work has not yet actualized itself and still always becoming, it is not yet an end result of a process. Rather the notion of *reflection* in early German Romanticism, to take a cue from Walter Benjamin (1996, pp.116-200), is this: the singular unfolding of the Work in relation to the

Universal (a *singular Universal!)* is not yet complete. Its incompletion that bears in itself a remnant of an incalculable future cannot be grasped by a thetic, posited, predicative act of judgment. The unfolding of the work towards its Absolute is thus a simultaneous process of infinite interruption. The task of Criticism, that of releasing and unfolding the necessary closure of the singular work towards the very Idea of the Universal for which poetry is there is thus inseparably related (Lacoue Labarthe, Phillippe & Jean Luc Nancy 1988) with the notion of Literary Absolute that is its simultaneous un-doing, or interrupting of any completion. Since the work carries the remnant of the un-become, the question of literature for itself is not: 'what is the condition of possibility of a literary judgment?', for judgment of a work of art presupposes the work as a 'given presence', already finished product, an accomplished totality, a system of signification. Thus for the Romantics, literature is infinite becoming (Schlegel 2003, pp. 249-50) that does not yet belong to itself and that infinitely lacks itself. Literature is thus infinitely exiled, infinitely outside of itself, always exterior to itself; literature does *not* yet have its essence; it does not have its property of being of itself, its own home. It has since long fallen outside of itself, withdrawn from itself, forgotten itself. To become infinitely is to fall outside home and thereby to come back home: it is only by going away from Ithaca Odysseus may come back home. To come back home is to be able to reach 'what is' (*Essence*), or to reach to 'that is' ('entities presently given') which is its *very* own being.

Therefore even German Romantic's thinking of infinite becoming is always in sight of presence, a dream of a homeland. It is dream (in so far it is nothing but a dream) is infinite negation of itself. The Romantics grasped this phenomenon of auto-negation as "irony". It opens the movement of a lost presence that is always *in sight* of its coming to presence. Despite its radicalism, despite its critique of the present, despite its attempted opening towards the future, the Romantic always adhered to a past that is more enchanting than all that is present, but an ideal past whose return would alone constitute its future, its *telos*. In the case of the Romantics, this adherence to the past political existence, not positively, not in relation to a *in-itself*, can end up in a reactionary politics, in the very ironical manner that is singular to the Romantics that infinitely negates what it sneers as the everyday banality of bourgeois political closure. Politically, it is the faithfulness to a past political system, grand, heroic and sublime, which is in the possession of the few aristocratic individuals. However, as an interruption of any given, the Romantic predicament is that of an aporia to the utmost limit which is summed up in Schlegel's fragment: 'It is equally fatal for the mind to have a system and to have none' (Ibid., p. 247). It is as if an essential experience of poetry can henceforth only be aporetic and undecidable. It must combine demands which refuse combination and commensuration: the demand of system and to have none, the demand of foundation and demand of its interruption, the demand of the Absolute and the demand of an infinite irony, the demand to contest every other totality, and but also the demand to contest its own ground on the basis of which contestation is carried on. As if literature, in its infinite contestation, can only negate itself only because it must contest everything. From this Hegel brings this logic to its devastating result: the disappearance of poetry, the passing away of poetry; as if, in a necessary manner, poetry can only disappear, only because it is infinite becoming, an infinite coming to itself.

## VIII

What happens when the line—between two incommensurable demands—becomes undecidable? As if infinite contestation turns *aporetic*; becoming everything, it no longer becomes capable of positing its own ground, Being or substance. Here Maurice Blanchot's writings help us to think what is at stake when literature becomes everything that is possible (for that matter, nothing any more belonging to the order of possibility) and thereby not being able to be itself, to have its own essence belonging to itself. The work of art interrupts, creates a void, or cuts away (Schelling 2000) into the given, into what is presently present. In this cutting away, in this creating a void into the very heart of what has become, literary work prepares for what is not yet, opens to the call of coming. The undecidability of the line is not nihilism, for it enables an infinite contestation, and affirms thereby the coming of the future. This is the messianic side of redemptive thinking that the infinite contestation must prepare the 'yes' saying to what must come, what is always there to come.

The task of the critic is to make manifest, to articulate this potency and this potentiality, this possibility of the work of arts, without making work of art a tool or a medium of a calculable programme for future. Letting the literary work, or artistic work its sheer *coming to presence*, in coming pure and simple without violence and reification, objectification or subjectification, the critic hints at the potency and the potentiality of this very coming, without seeking to exhaust its unnameable character that the artistic work of arts carries in its infinite becoming. All works of arts, in sheer *coming to presence*, in its pure and simple existing, carry what has not come to presence, what has not come to be in the name, the unnameable par excellence. Seeking to arrest this excess in the method-oriented scientific-technological interpretation, which is always borrowed from a certain dominant metaphysics is violence to the unnameable which each of the work of art carries. Literature thereby comes to be identifiable as a certain set of texts or works which can be classified, arranged and ordered like any other scientific discourses existing, or at best is seen as historical document that reveals what has become. The messianic intensity of affirming the coming, carried as potency in works of arts, is thereby subordinated to a document of what has become, to history. It is here Ernst Bloch's (1995) thoughts on works of arts are significant who sees in the works of art, not so much documents of an historical epoch that is finished, but the singular relation to coming, as sheer presencing that alone may redeem the unredeemed world.

## IX

In his *The Inoperative Community* (Nancy 1991), in response to Maurice Blanchot's *The Unavowable Community* (Blanchot 1983), Jean-Luc Nancy addresses what happens to community and society when literature, instead of representing the fullness of society's self-presence, introduces an incompletion, or Void. The community then, in Jean Luc Nancy's term, becomes "inoperative", and in Blanchot's term, "Unavowable": society or community that contests its own closure interminably, infinitely, unworking the 'mythic foundation' (Nancy 1991) of society so that society can remain open, unconditionally, to what is *to come*. Since literature is this infinite contestation, it cannot be subordinated to any normative task of reductive totalization. If literature refuses to subordinate itself to any given society or community's closure, it is because it is social in a more originary manner than that can be thought in terms of any reductive closure of *this* or *that* society. By transcending any habitation and name, literature opens each habitation and name to the not yet unconditionally in an unconditional hospitality. In this manner literature discontinues and departs from its self-presence, forever erasing itself, and thereby opening itself to the messianic intensity of coming.

# *Martin Heidegger and the Question of the Theologico-Political*

## I

At stake here is the theologico-political question of finitude. The problematic that is the matter of thinking here as the 'theologico-political' is, in a certain manner, to be distinguished from, though having a certain relation to, what is commonly known in recent scholarship and critical thinking as 'political theology'. Under the rubric of the theologico-political the question of secularism and its criticism is not posed as a question concerning the juridico-political. As a term that is used in recent scholarship and critical discourses, 'political theology' has a conceptual history, mainly associated with the name Carl Schmitt. In recent scholarship and critical discourses, 'political theology' or even 'economic theology' (there can be more of such theologies) seem to have become something like areas of investigation, or regional domains of investigation. Hence one may speak of, for example, an 'economic theology', related to, but distinguished from 'political theology'.

On the other hand what is called here as 'the theological-political', which is distinguished from 'political theology', at least in the given sense of what is called 'political theology', is not one of the regional domains of investigation, though like political theology (I am here using Carl Schmitt's sense), it is concerned with the problematic connection between theology and the political, but one that is *not* pertaining to the juridico-political dimension alone. Instead what is attempted here, with Heidegger and against him, an interrogation of what I am calling 'theologico-political', which has a resonance with what Martin Heidegger calls 'onto-theology'. Here both 'theological' and 'political' receive different determinations than the given senses —of which nothing much can be said here, given the limited concern of this article—differences of determinations that are not merely differences between two different regions called 'theological' and 'political'. The interrogation of the theological political, which is the main concern here, does not advance anything like a claim of 'secularism'. This claim or disclaim of 'secularism' demands a far more fundamental, therefore not belonging to any regional investigation.

What is called theologico political here refers, therefore, to a certain *gesture*, or *style* of thinking rather than a regional domain of thinking; this style of thinking is something like, due to lack of a better term, I shall call ' quasi-transcendental' thinking: a provisional term that I am willing to discard. It is concerned with the history of a concept that is constitutive of a discourse, instead of analysing the specificity of a given historical period. Such a concept that concerns us here is the question of finitude. With the question of finitude as guiding question, I will attempt to examine its complex relation to the theologico-political where what at stake is the very notion of 'finitude' and 'theologico-political'. Hence neither "finitude" nor 'theologico-political' are problems that are 'given presences'. These problematics are interrogated not as problematics that are already there but what will be problematized, what will become names of problems, questions, and stakes. Therefore this article is only a preliminary study, an attempted opening of a world of investigations to come, opening to the undecidable and incalculable results, without an end in view yet, and therefore subject to revisions, renewals, or perhaps even abandonment. It is a provisional gesture of thinking, a certain deconstructive style of reading of what constitutes or de-constitutes the dominant metaphysical determination of the political and the theological. Therefore these determinations do not have such a well-defined contour such as 'political theology': they are to be elaborated on the path of thinking. In this sense they are to be considered as marks on the pathway of thinking. The marks are to be invented, beyond the given, so that they give a certain orientation to thinking, which does not exclude the possibility of disorientation of the path. Therefore creative thinking always demands re-inventions of gestures, re-marking the path of thinking, re-marking and de-marking of what is marked. This de-marking is at once a de-marcation that gives severity, simplicity, and certain sobriety to our thinking if thinking has to sustain itself and to give itself time, time to mark, re-mark, de-mark and demarcate itself.

Let me return. The 'political' in the phrase 'theologico-political' that is questioned here is to be distinguished from what we think in the name or concept as "politics". The latter is the juridico-legislative manner of thinking the communal life where the political existence of the community takes the State as the modality: this is applicable even if the nation state nowadays is supposed to be, rightly or wrongly, withering away, in the age of certain globalization. I am not going to elaborate the question of the State in its complex relation to Nation-State, which is not really my concern here. Instead 'political' here is to be understood as the metaphysical determination of communication life or political existence, which for example Plato calls *Politeia,* which in English translation came to be known as the book *Republic.* Plato never calls his book by the name *Republic,* the name perhaps is unknown to him. Instead he calls it *Politeia*: a metaphysical inquiry, or metaphysical determination of a communal existence, which I shall call *political,* political of which the innermost, essential characteristics, its being—I say 'essential' and 'innermost' that is to be distinguished from the dominant notion of 'essence'—is *being-towards-each others* as the essential comportment of Being itself . The essential knowledge of it is grasped in a constellation of *Ideas,* of what Plato calls *Eidos:* this constellation of *Ideas* in which and by means of which the essential knowledge of the communal existence is grasped is what came to be known as *Philosophy.* In modern philosophy this metaphysics of the political is transformed into the ontological and theological determinations in their interrelations to each other: this is what is meant as 'Onto-Theology' by Heidegger in his lecture called *The Onto-Theological Constitution of Metaphysics.* Therefore both ontological and theological, in their innermost interrelation, belong together to metaphysics: they concern the Ground of Being, or Being as Ground. In Heidegger's reading of the history of this metaphysics, it is Hegel who wanted to accomplish this metaphysics and bring it to a closure, who grasped this Ground dialectically-historically. Therefore the dialectical-historical determination of the political existence, at least in Hegelian form, is a giving ground, which also means giving an account of the ground, or grounding onto-theologically, that means Being as the ground of Being's *being-towards-each other*. This ground is apprehended, represented in the form of logical Judgment, which is different from a formal logic, in predicative proposition that *apophantically* grasps, or recuperates. Recuperates what?: the *giving* of ground that first of all comes presence, since for Hegel this ground does not pre-exist . Thus in Hegel, the ground of Being's being-towards-each-other *comes to presence in coming of the ground to itself. This coming of the ground to itself is the question of finitude, since there nothing precedes this coming. The nothingness of the preceding is grasped as finitude.*

I will not be able to elaborate here the immense history of the notion of finitude in modern philosophy. We have to begin with Kant who saw finitude as the question concerning the very possibility and impossibility of metaphysics and the impossibility of Absolute self-grounding, as a result of which practical reason can only appear as regulative principle which can only be approximated given the infinite time, or a time outside time. As a result the absolute self-grounding is infinitely postponed, because of finitude that marks the mortal. So it is transformed by Fichte for whom finitude is *self-positing* of the Ego in the primordial act of coming to itself out of nothing, a process with an unconditional beginning, as with Kant, never accomplishing its self-grounding. In other words, if I am allowed to say this, modern philosophy is marked by the birth of the notion of finitude. Hegel, whose profound indebtedness to Fichte only recently has come to be acknowledged, has transformed Fichtean self-positing of the Ego out of finitude, or rather where finitude itself is this self-positing, Hegel transformed it into the self-grounding coming to presence of being-towards-each other as essential of our dialectical-historical existence. *It is therefore the notion of finitude, as the coming to presence of Being's being-towards-each-other as historically coming of political existence—is a theological and ontological notion. Since the onto-theological belong together to metaphysics, finitude is a metaphysical notion par excellence: it concerns the giving ground out of the groundless—of what comes to presence:* Theo *as the permanent and* Being *as the Universal ground of beings.* After Hegel, perhaps already with Kant, the metaphysical determination of our political existence is therefore a finite thinking: Hegel calls this finite thinking 'speculative', by which he means 'historical' re-appropriation of the Same, or historical re-appropriation of a self-foundational ground. The self-foundational ground of the historical-political existence, presupposing *nothing* transcendent outside, arising out of a ground that is pure negativity, is grasped by Hegel as self-foundational unity of a logical judgment. Our historical-political existence as being-towards-each-other is to ground itself, to give itself its ground, to come to itself—without any transcendent ground—out of the groundless, as if out of death. *This death must work, which is death's supreme work, to give ground to our historico-political existence.* The work of death is the metaphysical activity of the giving ground of our historico-political existence. Therefore Hegel can make this tremendous claim in his *Logic*: '*Being is ... Nothing*'(Hegel 1975, p. 126). What death gives, which is the gift of death, is the ground of Being, Being's *being-towards-itself-and-to-each-other.* As the ground of Being, or Being as the ground, death is each time onto-theological. The question of finitude and death is therefore the metaphysically constitutive of the theologico-political, which means, the political is founded on a non-foundation, in the absence of any already present foundation. *Instead of God constituting the theologico-political as the supreme ground, for there is no more divine right of the King as the saying goes, whether for right or wrong, the death of God itself serves as the ground.*

This theological ground without *theo*, since God himself must come to himself through his very nothingness, suffering the agony of mortality: this tremendous power of nothingness is a power unlike any other power. The sovereignty of this power is this power that is nothing, born out of nothing, but it is more powerful than any other power: this power is the power of sovereign decision, because sovereign decisions are always taken at the limit, that disrupt any given normative order of general validity. The moment of decision is the moment which performs the work of death, in that it nullifies any given ground, and makes this void itself a labour of giving ground. Therefore the metaphysical essence of ground, constitutive of a certain speculative-political existence, is a finite experience. This labour is the giving ground out of nullity where decisions are taken at the limit, where promise is seen in danger. The theologico-political has therefore this intimate connection with certain decisionism, for decisionism presupposes this state (which is statelessness), a decisionism which operates as the very metaphysical determination of the political: it wants to convert —as Hegel says famously in *Phenomenology of Spirit*—the nothingness into Being.

## II

It has already been remarked of Heidegger's attempted *step back* from *the onto-theological constitution of metaphysics*. To think of the question of Being, and later after the *Kehre* the question of truth in relation to the history of metaphysics is to think, at the end of metaphysics, non-onto-theologically. If that is so, the whole task of *Being and Time, Kant and the Problem of Metaphysics* along with his lectures on *The Fundamental Concepts of Metaphysics:* this whole task of 'destruction of ontology' and to think the question of Being anew will be problematic and questionable, as if the whole edifice of Heidegger's early works are under the danger of self-refutation. Heidegger's two fold tasks in *Being and Time,* the tasks which he takes further into his *Kantbuch* and other texts around that time, take *finitude* as the essential horizon of thinking. Is this the reason of a certain decisionism in Heidegger, and if one jumps too quickly, for we should be aware of any such jumps? Does this decisionism also explain his own theologico-political at the unforgivable level of joining a fascist party? Is this also the reason that later Heidegger supposed to have left behind, if Henri Birault's (Birault 1960; Derrida 1978, p. 407) reading of Heidegger is acceptable, the very notion of finitude, since it is at least still ontologically theological, the very onto-theological that Heidegger attempts to deconstruct? *The deconstruction of the onto-theological thus has remained onto-theological itself, at least ontologically theological.* The Heideggerian task of the 'destruction of ontology' is permeated by the very onto-theology, which in Heidegger's writings of that terrible period, appears as *'the metaphysics of Dasein'*, Germans as the metaphysical people who must give themselves a historical destiny. A people giving itself a destiny, a task which demands decision and firm resolution is the metaphysical task of the people that gather into unity of a decision its political, its Being as being-towards-each-other. The devout Christian school boy who renounced his Christianity in order to be philosopher, for philosophy is not compatible with Christianity: does the renounced theology not appear again in the new metaphysical task of the historical Dasein, and later in his old days in the guise of a new theologico-poetic, in the notion of *Holy* and welcoming of the Divine in the poetic saying? Are we not going too fast here?

In 1929 in Davos there took place a disputation between Martin Heidegger and Ernst Cassirer on interpretation of Kant's *Critique of Pure Reason* . Though it appears at first as differences of interpretations of Kant, the profound philosophical-political implications of the disputation have never been seriously discussed. For Cassirer, the finitude of the mortals requires of a truth outside, transcendence so that the mortal may not enclose himself in the most dangerous immanence. Therefore Cassirer suspects a danger, though not explicitly articulated, in the new metaphysics of *angst* of Dasein holding out to its nothingness, where Dasein acquires hardening of a resolute self-assertion in the face of its own nothingness. Heidegger, on the other hand, makes the most paradoxical assertion that the very nothingness of Dasein itself is Dasein's ecstatic transcendence, that is, his finitude. Dasein itself each time is transcendence in so far as Dasein is finite, in an essential and innermost manner. What is it to say that the transcendence of Dasein is its finitude? To understand this it is necessary to go through the entirety of *Being and Time*, along with the *Kantbuch* and the controversial *What is Metaphysics?*. Thus in his disputation with Cassirer, Heidegger says:

> ... It must be shown that: because man is the creature who is transcendent, i.e. who is open to beings in totality and to himself, that through this eccentric character man at the same time also stands within the totality of beings in general...which leads man back beyond himself and into the totality of beings in order to make manifest to him there, with all his freedom, the nothingness of Dasein. (Heidegger 1997, p. 204).

It is the manifestation of the nothingness of Dasein that ecstatically holds him outside of himself and opens to beings in totality: this ecstasy, which is its transcendence, is decisive for Dasein, for decision is at each moment must be ecstatic. Here comes the critique of Hegel, the whole stake of Heideggerian 'destruction of ontology', of the dominant metaphysical tradition that finds its onto-theological-fulfilment in Hegel: that what is missing in the Hegelian onto-theological notion of finitude, which Hegel metaphysically grasped as negativity, on the basis of which Hegel built up the immense apparatus or system of the historico-political, what is missing in this speculative determination of the historico-political, is none but a theological ontology, is *decision*. A fundamental ontology must therefore introduce a 'destruction of ontology' so that decision is thought anew, no longer in relation to negativity, but to Nothing, a non-negative nothing. Therefore the whole question of finitude is be thought anew, a finitude which is Nothing of Dasein is the overcoming of the onto-theological notion of finitude, so that overcoming of the onto-theological constitution of metaphysics may lead to think of metaphysics itself more essentially and fundamentally. In other words, the notion of decision itself is to be metaphysically decided, but no longer as the metaphysics of onto-theology, but as metaphysics of Dasein. The Heideggerian thinking of the German people as metaphysical, and the metaphysics of people presupposes this metaphysics of finitude, Dasein's essential Nothingness, which in each case decides for itself its essential destiny, its metaphysical fate. The destinal, or fateful movement of a metaphysical people is its nothingness: only a fateful people on the basis, or on the absence of any given basis, of nothingness can bring to itself its authentic historical decision, which is destinal, its metaphysical fate. Thus Hölderlin, Schelling and Nietzsche, along with Heraclitus are evoked in this tremendous *polemos* of lightening and darkening of Being, as adversaries against Hegel's onto-theological metaphysics. Therefore it is not even surprising that this polemos evokes the divine and the Holy in later Heidegger: here art becomes the place where placing as such—which Heidegger calls *the Open*—takes place. This time *timing*, and space *spacing* is essentially an experience of mortality, of nothingness. Hegel is again the adversary here: for according to Heidegger, in Hegelian metaphysics time does not time, and space does not space. Therefore there is no face-to-face encounter in Hegel, which means there is no decision in Hegel. I should better say that according to Heidegger there is a decision in Hegel which is not decisive enough; it is not originary enough, which is not metaphysical enough. Therefore metaphysics must be overcome, not to leave behind metaphysics as such, but to bring metaphysics to its decisive, originary task for the first time.

Thus we see the whole disturbing aporetic relation of theological to the political, which from Spinoza has occupied the philosophers. What has disturbed Heidegger, also Feuerbach, about Hegelian dialectical-historical is its theological foundation, a political that is ontologically founded by the theological—that is, no longer the theological as 'given presence', but as sheer unrest negativity. The place of theological is aporetic and disturbing, which Spinoza, before many others so intensely experienced: the violence and closure of the theologically founded political. *Yet on the other hand it is seen—as in Heidegger's case here—each time there is an attempt to think of the political beyond any theological foundation, it either repeats the theological foundation in a new guise, or it ends up by evoking a new metaphysics of the people, which shows the shallowness of the claims for secularism that is supposing to be, or to have taken place.* A critique of the theological political, which is the very task in Heideggerian thinking, then has to take place beyond the keen of a fundamental ontology, without evoking thereby "secularism" at least in the given sense of the term.

## III

In later Heidegger there takes place subtle changes that are almost imperceptible even to keenest readers of Heidegger. It is no longer *Anxiety as the fundamental mood of Dasein, but a fundamental attunement of mourning, or melancholy that permeates Heidegger's last works.* Instead of the anxious Dasein's resolute, even virile and heroic self-assertion of its very being-towards-death, it's very impossibility of its possibility to be, mournfulness or a sadness comes to be the fundamental attunement of the mortal existence. Thus it is language, especially of poetic Saying, in its intimate connection with mortality, appears as gift. Like his mortality for the mortal, the language is not the possession of the one who speaks. Thus the fundamental task of the political, thought in a more originary manner, is no longer the virile, heroic assertion of his very nothingness, but renunciation of possession or mastery. Renunciation always attunes us with a certain sadness, which is neither accidental pessimism, nor a calculated risk, but the fundamental attunement of existence. It bespeaks the essential mortality of the mortals, his originary finitude which is that of man's never being able to reach his own self-grounding even in his nothingness. In this recognition of the mortality of the mortals and his finitude: there alone lies the nobility of man, recognition of man's requirement to renounce appropriation of his own ground, which means, accepting man's mortality as mortality.

Redemption of the theological-political violence therefore cannot occur at the level of constituting for a people a metaphysical self-foundation out of finitude, but renunciation of any mastery of one's ground. Melancholy attunes us when the finite being recognizes his finitude and this noble recognition enables renunciation of violence.

## IV

The theological-political has thus remained an open question. It points towards not only difficulty of conceiving so-called secular politics, it also asks us to think of the political in a more originary manner, not merely limited to the juridico-legislative domain. Instead it concerns the very possibility or impossibility of an ontological foundation of our being towards each other. At stake, finally, is the necessity to think of the place of violence that often lies at the labour of founding a political existence, or a communal existence. The melancholy or sadness that has remained unredeemed in our dialectical-historical political existence demands of a time yet to come. Heidegger thus, towards the end of his life, attempts to think the place of language is the welcoming of the arriving, which is the promise of language. Language is not what the mortal man appropriates because he speaks, but language, first disappropriating man, endows him with the gift of speech. To be able to speak is not capacity, nor mastery, but an affirmation of a time to arrive. Therefore only a finite being like man is endowed with language, because he knows his death as death, in-appropriable death, death that does not serve the power that masters. This non-masterable death attunes us with a fundamental sadness. This is not nihilism nor pessimism, but an attempt to think of the political anew. If Heidegger is discussed here, it is because of this very aporetic of his philosophy: the danger and the promise that his philosophy offers.

# *Is Freedom the First Right?*[*]

## I

Beyond the violence of historical closure: this is the place of language as gift to the infinite other and an intimation of redemption. By showing the limit of this historical closure, the exigency of thinking another modality of time is recognized which is otherwise than historical time of negativity. History is put into question by the coming of the otherwise, and is thereby redeemed. This redemption of history is not without judgment: it is the judgment of the Other, the redeeming transcendence irreducible to the ontological time of immanence. We shall interrogate here the closure of a dominant philosophical determination of freedom where freedom is always freedom *to be*, let's say ontological freedom, where it is understood in a certain relation to a certain understanding of Reason which the self-conscious humanity produces as history through the negative labour of the concept. Here the task of freedom is that of constituting the anonymous, faceless order of Universality, a system of relations, a totality of rationalized institutions without singularities, a generalized order of a homogeneous economy where each of the homogenized particular limits the other particulars through negation.

---

* This paper was read at a conference on " Moral Dilemmas in the Globalized World", held at the Centre for Philosophy, School of Social Sciences, I, Jawaharlal Nehru University, February 27-29, 2008.

Here the universality accomplishes itself as self-same Same: this autonomy—that means freedom *to be* itself—is autonomy accomplished through and as reconciliation. This reconciliation is also thought to be the healing of the wound of history, healing the tears and pains of the labour of the concept, healing the violence of the thetic which the labour of the concept itself, at each moment of coming to itself, posits.

It is necessary to ask whether the wound of history, the tears and violence of the concept is redeemed within the generalized economy of the History itself, or whether the requirement of redemption requires a coming outside this generalized economy of the Same, an intensification of the coming of the other, which thereby must exceed the economy of the freedom *to be*, but be a justice to the other, a redeeming justice? Thus freedom— understood as the self-grounding movement of the Subject that suffers violence at its own hand—as Hegel beautifully says—may not have priority to justice, since requirement of redemption is not fulfilled therein, thereby pointing towards either another thinking of freedom, or a notion of justice beyond freedom. It is necessary to think this question again in an age when universality—in the name of 'globalisation'—has not redeemed the wound of history, nor has freed us towards reconciliation beyond violence, where the singularity of the other is foreclosed and enclosed within a false immanence of generalized economy of the Same and economy for the Same.

## II

If the dominant metaphysics of the Subject that asserts the freedom *to be* itself has assumed, in Hegel's hand, the immanent closure of history, it thereby is not being able to redeem the suffering and violence of the historical existence, in so far as it knows no other redemption apart from the Concept, in so far as concept—because it emerges into itself only by positing itself —is itself an act, a labour of negation. The violence of the negativity, therefore, does not know true mourning, for it knows not death beyond negation, in so far as it knows of redemption only as reconciliation immanent to the economy of negativity. Therefore the melancholy of the historical existence is not consoled in the universality of concept, because for the concept death is mere "naught". The unredeemed mourning for a death which is not mere "naught", therefore, remains a remnant outside the universal realm of history where the freedom is realized, actualised and accomplished through the rationalized institutions. Since these rationalized institutions which constitute the realm of the juridico-political, hope not to presuppose anything outside the immanent closure of the Historical present, render themselves deaf to the claim of redemption and justice outside violence, the claim of transcendence of the coming of the other. Each time the concept — even the Concept of all concepts as infinite negativity—attempts to heal the sufferings and wound of history, it forgets the event of justice, or the event of redemption, or the event of its birth, which itself does not belong to the order of the Concept, the order of the universal generality. As a result the universal order of History, where the concept realizes the freedom *to be*, remains a not yet justice enough, not yet redeeming enough, since by an ineluctable logic, the Concept must not presuppose anything outside negativity, outside immanence. Therefore redemption in justice is an affirmation outside negativity, a non-negative affirmation towards transcendence irreducible to the juridico-political realm of historical actualisation, not rendering the juridico-political realm superfluous, but precisely demanding, requiring the juridico-political realm of historical freedom in the name of redemption, or justice. There remains this caesura—between the juridico-political realm of freedom and the redemptive justice, between the immanence of negativity and transcendence of a non-negative affirmation— since all acts of realizing freedom within a historical presence, or self-presencing remains finite, since there remains something yet to be realized, something transcendent outside which is anticipated in a messianic hope, the other to come which is not yet. This 'not yet'—this word that Ernst Bloch has articulated with such resonance of dignity and intensity of urgency—does not completely belong to history, since it is an non-negative affirmation of coming, an opening which remains beyond death, a time of redemption that will not come to pass, but must remain outside what has arrived. Every time the universal history, through the rational institutions, posits itself as negativity to ensure the right or freedom of the Same, it already produces asymmetry of its own realization and redemptive justice that exceeds it, so that an opening remains open to the coming of the not yet, which is outside the self-grounding movement of the Concept or the historical-dialectical Subject. Redemption remains coming, remains yet to come.

## III

What remains as remnant, and thus requires redemption, is justice. If freedom is necessary and if it is necessary to put into work all the rational institutions, it is not because freedom derives its signification from itself alone and be self-sufficient but rather because there is another time of justice that requires freedom to be effectuated in terms of law through juridical, political, economic institutions so that the violence that freedom risks to assume is put into question and remain open to the not yet.

It is not that the effectuation of freedom through the rational institutions is not necessary and that philosophical-political decisions are always arbitrary and would rather be discarded any form action that would transform the existing historical institutions. *This is rather to say that freedom is possible—freedom understood as rational effectuation of philosophical-political decisions through institutions—only when decision, singular each time, exceeds the very ontological determinability, exceeds the grounding on any a priori, calculative future for the Same or any absolute, auto-effectuating, auto-engendering historical negating subject.* Every time there occurs the singularity of judgment, it is history itself that is judged so that the singularity of the judgment must be an opening to an opening, to the promise of the 'not yet', to an exterior, irreducible incalculability which itself does not have its ontological grounding.

In his great work called *Inquiry into the Essence of Human Freedom*, Schelling calls freedom itself as opening, or '*releasing*'. Freedom must be released, or freedom releases beyond any immanent totality in order to open to a coming. This attempt to think anew freedom is no longer to be understood as negativity's act of grounding itself, as if over an abyss. Instead of appearing freedom as the property of the human, freedom enables and opens to the coming to presence by *releasing* this opening. Only through *releasement* the God or the mortal is opened to the coming of the otherwise. Schelling calls this experience 'intimation': it is an opening—not to Being as traditional ontology understood it, which found its accomplishment in the system of Hegel—but an opening to, what Schelling calls 'over-being' or 'beyond Being' (*Überseyn*). If the notion of freedom to be retained, either it is to be opened up to redemptive justice beyond Being or the metaphysics of Subjectivity, to Justice irreducible to the Universal order of anonymous Reason, or Freedom itself to be thought anew—without bringing the notion of justice—no longer as self-grounding act of the Subject through negativity, but over and beyond Being, and therefore as transcendence in intimation of the coming of redemption of history itself, where Reason, realizing its limit, opens to another freedom, to an actuality without potentiality. Later is the very task of Schelling's later philosophy. In both ways freedom—understood as the self-grounding act of rationality—is no longer recognized as the first right. In this way the question of responsibility itself is opened up anew as ethical question of justice in an age of globalization, when it is felt, more urgently than ever, that the juridico-politic of reconciliation is to be opened up towards an ethics of redemption, which means affirmation of future, of a coming time.

# *The Wound of the Negative*[*]

## I

This essay hopes to articulate the limit of the dialectical thought that attempts to bring together, and sublate the antagonistic, conflictual structure of community that is constituted at the peril of this opposition between "public" and "private". This opposition which dialectical thought seeks sublation (*Aufhebung*) can be shown to be as old as the very inception of the dominant metaphysical determination of the West: the opposition between *speech* and *voice* which from Aristotle to Rousseau and to Hegel is thought to be the very foundation of *Polis*. The sublation of this opposition can't but be *tragic*, that means such an act of sublation must pass through certain experience of death or dissolution, or even the peril of being: this is what (Hegel's) the speculative philosophy discovers, which is also the philosophy of the tragic. Thus the distinction or rather opposition between pleasure and pain on the one hand, and just and unjust on the other—which Aristotle determines to be the definition of the concept of the *political* par excellence –is inseparable from the question of language, of death and that of tragedy.

---

* This paper was read at a conference on "Public Sphere: The Fate of a Philosophical Concept", organized by the Indian Institute of Technology, New Delhi, India on March 21, 2006.

Taking Maurice Blanchot's non-dialectical notion of the worklessness of dying as a point of departure, I argue for the necessity of thinking outside the tragic-speculative determination of community, that means, outside the movement of a thinking that must pass through the oppositions between "private" and "public" as perilous moments of an auto-generative and autochthonous universal reason. The task of thinking thus that arises is not of a predicative structure of a community where the voice dies away and speech emerges as work, as *polis*; it is rather that of opening to the unconditionality of the immemorial which is more originary than "private" and "public". This excess of the immemorial is not more anymore "public" than "private"; it is rather the structural opening of each discourse that can never be "avowed" enough, yet in the name of which any concept of the *political* as such makes sense at all. Such a community is neither a well-definable civil society nor an Absolute state, but, what Maurice Blanchot calls, 'the unavowable community', the community destined to worklessness without destination.

## II

*At stake here is not so much, and not merely the distinction between "public" and "private" but, as we will see soon, the very concept of the* political *itself as such that will play the predominant part here, so that one can say that these twin concepts ("private" and "public") are the indexes to raise the very concept of the political itself anew. This is so far as these twin concepts presuppose a certain metaphysical grounding of the* political *that has determined our sense of the political and ethical for so long, as long as the inception of that metaphysics itself. This should be able to suggest, as far as possible here, that the concept of the metaphysical itself in its innermost ground of occidental reason is essentially a* political *one. This paper attempts to reveal the metaphysical structure of the concept of the political—of which "private" and "public" play a seminal part—in order to open this structure to new possibilities beyond the closure of such metaphysics. For that purpose, let me begin with Aristotle, with a certain well-recognized passage that occurs in* Politics,

> Nature, as we often say, makes nothing in vain, and man is the only animal whom she has endowed with the gift of speech. And whereas mere voice is but an indication of pleasure and pain and is therefore found in other animals (for their nature attains to the perception of pleasure and pain and the intimation of them to another, and no further), the power of speech is intended to set forth the expedient, and therefore likewise the just and unjust. And it is characteristics of man that he alone has any sense of good and evil, of just and unjust, and the like, and the association of living beings who have this sense makes a family and a state. (Aristotle 2001; 1253a, 8–18; p. 1129).

At stake in these lines is neither that of being concerned with the *political* nor with the metaphysical par say, but with the metaphysical grounding of a certain concept of the political as such. The political as such has as its end whose end-character is defined metaphysically and anthropologically, understood more fundamentally than what we generally understand by 'the anthropological'. Man is that being who not only has voice but s/he who judges, with his gift of speech, the good in contradiction to the evil, the just in contradiction to unjust. Now this is the metaphysical foundation of the concept of the political. The task of the political is to elevate—for Hegel this concept has the sense of *Aufhebung*—one 'thing' into the other: voice into speech, pleasure and pain into just and unjust, nature into the political. There is no politics in the domain of voice, in the ineffable realm of the poetry of pleasure and pain; politics begins precisely at that moment, at that point where the voice dies away and speech is born, which is the *logos of the political*, the logos where the ineffability of the immediate and the whims of the "private", through its very character of nullity that is "proper" to it, passes into the universality of logos: only then man is what he truly is – *the political being* par excellence.

## III

To put it simply, I would like to understand here the two statements whose meanings follow from Aristotle's words,

> —We shall see soon that this distinction, a very foundational one for

the concept of the *political,* between pleasure and pain (immediately associated with voice) and just and unjust (immediately connected with speech) is based upon certain thanatological determination of negativity as *work. The political* is the conception of work: politics *works*; it works as the work of the transformation of the one into the other; it transforms voice into speech, and pleasure (and pain) into just (and unjust). This transformation lies in the very structure of human language itself: language itself transforms, and thus is a work, voice into speech, and this work of transformation/metamorphosis is essentially negative one, as if in language voice itself must die away giving place to language (speech), as if death itself assumes a different meaning each time: death that is mere nature, natural death and death that is condition of the political as such. Death itself is thus not merely a natural death, for natural death is not any more political than a natural life. But death itself to be political, or if it must condition the event of the political, death must not merely *scream* but must itself *speak. Now, the question of the distinction between "public" and "private" is only intelligible within this metaphysical determination of the political.* If the dominant metaphysical determination of man is not merely the animal that *screams* but *speaks,* it is determined as such only so far as death itself must be able to *speak* and not merely *scream.* In Hegel's philosophy, this problematic occurs most sharply when he raises the question of the ethical order: the human community must be able to *sublate,* through the dialectical-speculative *representation* of death, the contradiction of the merely finite existence, the disparate realms of the private individuals, the *mute-screaming* of an immanent life, its lamentations and mourning on the one hand, and the discursive-*speaking* of the infinite on the other hand where speech tears open the closure of the merely individual, private insistence on the immediate.

— That this dialectical-speculative representation of death is inseparably bound up, at least in the case of Hegel, with the representational determination of the *tragic,* or rather a certain tragic determination of *representation.* The work of death must be able make the community possible so that community not merely *screams* but *speaks.* The definition of community for Hegel is essentially political: animals that have only voice, neither have they community nor they know anything like the political. Thus the *logos* of community is understood by Hegel as essentially that of the universal order of speech into which voice keeps vanishing away, passing into speech, the *logos* which is shared by anyone and everyone because it appears as Day where everything is intelligible and everything is "public". But this 'passing away' of voice into speech has nothing harmless and peaceful about it; it can only be violent and tragic one which Hegel grasps with the *agonal* concept of the dialectical. *The logos of the political is an agonal one and tragic.* The claim of the voice that finds the imposition of speech as violent and coercive is the claim of the ineffable: the dialectical mediation between them can thus only be tragic and agonal, a logic which Hegel expounds in his *Phenomenology of Spirit* when he evokes Sophocles' Antigone. Hegel's dialectics is based upon the insight that there can be no *immediate* identity of community with its inner essence; it can only be mediated through representation. This representation is a tragic one. Tragic here works like Aristotelian *Catharsis*: through tragedy the torn community is redeemed, the sufferings borne of the *sacrifices* (community that renews itself through sacrifices[1], by means of *War*[2]) are healed. The ethical community, through these agonal and tragic conflicts, must point towards its resolution which Hegel names *Aufhebung:* that one must be able *speak* through his death, beyond his death by transfiguring his death itself as tragic work. Through dying of voice, voice itself receives a renewed life which is *speech.*

Which means that, and this is the final point,

— One must be able to die in order to speak, but in order to speak one must not be dying. My paper dwells on this dialectical impasse of mimesis - the double demands that at the same time separates its own simultaneity, disrupts its speaking to itself, carrying over the suffering of the scream (it's too much screaming arises out of its not being able to speak enough, being already smothered by its own absence, by its own death): this dying and not able to die persists with a perseverance that is never sublated, that does not know *Aufhebung.* Taking Blanchot's distinction of death and dying as a clue, I would argue that it is essentially a question of speaking and screaming: at the very moment of community's realization of its *Aufhebung,* the suffering of the scream never ceases screaming, even at the absolute realization of speech and its sense. The result —which itself would not know knowledge—is that the community never reaches complete *Aufhebung,* the tragic resolution and atonement. In other words, the sublation of the "private" and "public", "particular" and "universal", "voice" and "speech" will never be accomplished or achieved; the ethical order of community would forever be haunted by the spectre of the outside (outside these distinctions) that would in advance un-work the domain of the political. This wound would not know its *Aufhebung* in sense or speech: a wound without *Catharsis*, because it is the wound of negativity without concept; it is an excess, excess of any dialectical sublation, beyond any immanent closure, a scream beyond the negativity of speculative representation: it is the dying of the other whose dying is un-sacrificiable, a remnant and remaining, opening time itself to the coming one.

## IV

Let us read Aristotle again,

> Nature, as we often say, makes nothing in vain, and man is the only animal whom she has endowed with the gift of speech. And whereas mere voice is but an indication of pleasure and pain and is therefore found in other animals (for their nature attains to the perception of pleasure and pain and the intimation of them to another, and no further), the power of speech is intended to set forth the expedient, and therefore likewise the just and unjust. And it is characteristics of man that he alone has any sense of good and evil, of just and unjust, and the like, and the association of living beings who have this sense makes a family and a state. (Aristotle 2001; 1253a, 8–18; p. 1129)

A community (community that is determined to be such as far as community is not merely founded upon *pain* and *pleasure,* but upon *just* and *unjust*) must presuppose the distribution of *voice* and *speech*. This distribution has, however, remained fundamental to the dominant philosophical determination of what is called "community". What has become for Hegel of this distinction is the dialectical *contamination* of their infinite difference, no longer as *transcendental judgment*, but as *speculative judgment* (where subject and its predicate constantly swap its positions so that no fixity of their positions remains). This transformation into *speculative judgment* is accomplished (since it has to be *accomplished)* by introducing temporality, and thus introducing finitude (for dissolution of the fixity of the positions of the subject and predicate is dissolution as movement). Now, the judgment is essentially a work of positing. It will be interesting to note here the relationship that the very labour of judgment entails with the violence of *positing*, that has its own history, which, if we follow the dialectical rigour of speculative idealism, would be none other than itself, its excess, its *op-posit*. A community, based on this metaphysics of judgment, must respond to two demands, incommensurable, and yet at the same time: (1) to continuously posit violent oppositions, between "private" and "public", enemy and friendship, voice and speech etc, on the basis of which something called "politics" exists at all, and (2) to sublate once and for all these oppositions, and so as not to have the 'bad infinity' of continuously existing distinction of "private" and "public". Only then it will be truly speculative judgment which is unlike the transcendental judgment where the oppositions extend to infinity without resolutions. So the task of a dialectical thinking is bring resolution of the oppositions between "private" and "public", particular and universal, etc. This is Hegel's transformation of Kantian bad infinity into good infinity.

One can already see what I am pointing towards: a community, constituting itself on the dialectical modality of judgment, cannot successfully sublate the violence that lies in the very dialectics of judgment itself (thesis-antithesis-synthesis), even if its fundamental task is precisely to go beyond its violence. This means, by a necessary logic, it installs violence to heal violence. This is according to the old Aristotelian logic of Catharsis. The dialectical logic of judgment has the force of law, that of a power of dissolution and positing. Hence the community must appear to itself essentially as law, which concerns (as Hegel says) the dead individual and not the living. The supreme work of law is shown in its power of dissolution, in its absolute freedom of terror. As a result, the political animal must appear in his death by being first interpenetrated by the force of law. Man becomes political when his existence is traversed by the law of death and when he learns to maintain this work of death as work. The death of the voice is the beginning of speech, and, as we know, only a speaking animal is properly a political animal. For Hegel, thus, language is essentially a political work or work of the political: it makes politics possible, for politics is not essentially concerned with the pleasure and pain, but with just and unjust. In the ethical order language has for its content the essence of the community (while the legal status, it acquires the formal character): language sublates the disparate, disconnected, merely private, isolated and finite being that merely has a voice into the universality of speech. This sublation occurs as negation of the real as real, which means, by not being real, voice realizes its truth in speech of the community, as it were, voice dies away (and yet retained) so that speech takes place:

> It is the power of speech, as that which performs what has to be performed. For it is the real existence of the pure self as self; in speech, self-consciousness, *qua independent separate individuality*, comes as such into existence, so that it exists for others... language however, contains it in its purity, it alone expresses the 'I' the 'I' itself. This *real* existence of the 'I' is *qua* real existence, an objectivity which has in it the true nature of the 'I'. The 'I' is this particular 'I'— but equally the *universal* 'I'; it's manifesting is also at once the externalization and vanishing of *this* particular 'I', and as a result the 'I' remains in its universality. The 'I' that utters itself is *heard* or *perceived*; it is an infection in which it has immediately passed into unity with those for whom it is a real existence, and is a universal self-consciousness. That it is *perceived* or *heard* means that *its real existence dies away*; this its otherness has been taken back into itself; and its real existence is just this: that as a self-conscious Now, as real existence, it is *not* a real existence, and through this vanishing it *is* a real existence.(Hegel 1998, pp. 308-9)

If community has this essential relationship with speech, with language, it is this: that community is essentially linguistic. There is no community and no politics without language, because the distinction of *just* and *unjust* can only be made only by virtue of the human being gifted with the gift of speech. Death, which makes disappear of all that appears, seems to make all work workless and impotent, itself must appear to the very community's knowledge of itself as its inner truth, its inner movement, the immanent narrative of its self-becoming. Such knowledge is not possible without language. The community requires, for that matter, as its very possibility, the maintenance of what cannot be maintained[3]: death itself must be able to be present to itself. This maintenance of death is a movement (and not an arrest of movement): *the movement of* voice *dying* and *the emergence of* speech. In other words, community—speculative, in that it does not have its ground or foundation transcendent to it—must need spectacle, a theatrical representation. We see here that it is a tragic spectacle. The tragic spectacle allows death to be represented without anyone dying[4]. This means that the community demands feigned death, with the tacit knowledge already gathered that this death will not ruin anything anyone anymore; or rather it must be that death saves us ("we", "community" "people" who speak and not merely scream) from death—from the other death that brings disaster and ruins the works of the mortal in advance, that delivers the foundations of the community to slow dissipation and dissolution. That death must save community—the ethical order—from death: this is the homeopathic *catharsis* of the *tragic mimesis,* the *Aufhebung* of the dialectical paradigm of community that is founded on the *work of death*, on sacrifice and on the meaning of violence. But in that way, the other death—without meaning, sheer loss and its infinite disaster, as Blanchot (Blanchot 1995) points out itself escapes: it appears without appearing in the very work of language, not as speech qua speech, but as an incessant perseverance, in its refusing to die, of scream—of the other, what has remained of the other—the scream of language, beyond "private" and "public", is the undying death of the other.

Now I can bring to relief the point that I have been really trying to elaborate through a long detour. The task or the point is to open to the 'thought of the outside' beyond the dialectical oppositions between "private" and "public", "voice" and "speech", "particular" and "universal" and their resolutions. This opening the closure of the dialectical to the outside demands the works of deconstruction of the very metaphysical determination of the political as such.

## V

In the coming part of the article, I shall take up Hegel's *Phenomenology of Spirit*, especially that moment of Hegel's text where the agonal relationship between "public" and "private", between "universal" and "particular" assumes the most dramatic intensity, being the most tragic. It appears at that moment when these two domains, or better two modes of being assume the forms of two antagonistic laws. And it is interesting to observe that precisely here that there comes to be staged a tragic play: Sophocles' Antigone.

It is not for nothing that *Antigone* is discussed precisely at that moment in *Phenomenology of Spirit*—at the very heart of the text—when Spirit sublates its moments of Reason (these moments are: "The Certainty and the Truth of Reason", "The Actualization of Rational Self-Consciousness through its Own Activity", "Individuality Which Takes Itself to be Real in and for Itself") and appears as its first moment: "the True Sprit: The Ethical Order". It means: the question concerning the ethical order is already an actualization of reason. As actualized reason, the truth of reason is spirit. In other words, the question concerning the *wound* of the ethnical order, which is in question here, belongs to the dialectical stage of *spirit*, which is *actuality*, or substance in as much as substance is understood as the spiritual essence.[5] Thus Antigone's suffering is spiritual and belongs to the ethical order, which is already that of universal realm of actualizing substance. Though it is the universality of the spiritual realm to which the ethical order belongs, the ethical order is not yet conscious of its substance and hence, as in the previous shapes of spirit, it is marked by the dialectical contradiction of the two modes of being (corresponding to the two forms of law): the *private* individual being that justifies itself in the name of the immediate self-certainty of divine law and in the name of which it resists what it perceives to be the coercive power of the universal above it; and on the other hand, the universal itself that justifies itself in the name being able to elevate itself beyond the tyranny of the "natural" and the "immediate", of blood and soil, of voice and scream. Thus the *logos* of the universal has essentially the force or power of judgment: it wants to subjugate the primordial claims of the "natural" and "immediate" in the name of justice executed by the rational institutions such as State, etc. These 'public' rational institutions which from Aristotle to Hegel would be considered properly 'political', institutions which are founded upon the claim of the universal, demand obligation from individuals who otherwise would prefer to be enclosed in the immanence of self-certainty. Thus the simple spiritual substance is divided, rent asunder—precisely for its actualization—into human law as the universal law of the Day where everything is *public* (where all secrets will be considered tyrannical) and divine law as individual, mere *private* law of the elemental unconscious nature. As in Aristotle, this contradiction is that of the duality of "actuality" which belongs to the universal realm of spirit on the one hand, and "potentiality", which is yet to be actualized, the individual realm of sensuous existence on the other. Human law is *actual* in as much as it is universal through its power of the negative and the divine law is *potential* as that which is yet to be sublated into the universal world of human law. One can see that this division is not in which both sides are equally recognized: manhood, who as the human law of universality has already actualized/effectuated the potential which is to be seen in the real institutions in objective forms, the state and customs and in the discursive-speaking form of law, the sovereign law of universality that sublated what is the mere particular, private, animal existence of the individual through negativity, through the act of his own death. In other words, man is one who has effectuated/actualized his humanity through the negative-negating action by putting his mere, bare existence and his mere voice in risk; he has assumed the work of death, allowing death to pass through him as the force of law, and thus allowing himself to be transfigured him into the universal. Only thus he is the Subject of history. He is the power of the negative, the terror of the state who subsumes the individuals by waging war on them. As such, man is the worker who transforms the given bare existence, his mere voice to produce the universal order of reason. By negating his individual sensuous existence, through this death—which is its deed—man attains the universal status of "citizen".

The deed, then which embraces the entire existence of the blood-relation, does not concern the citizen, for he does not belong to the family, nor the individual who is to become a citizen and will cease to count this particular individual; it has as its object and content this particular individual who belongs to the family, but is taken as a universal being freed from his sensuous, i.e. individual, reality. The deed no longer concerns the living but the dead, the individual who, after a long succession of separate disconnected experiences, concentrates himself into a single completed shape and has raised himself out of the unrest of the accidents of life into the calm of simple universality. But because it is only as a citizen that he is actual and substantial, the individual, so far as he is not a citizen but belongs to the family, is only an unreal impotent shadow. (Hegel 1998, pp. 269-70)

The member of the state or the citizen is universal who has sublated his animal, irrational existence; this is his *work,* his deed and this work is *the work of negativity.* The universal citizen is the *Aufhebung* of disparate, unconnected particular existences into the self-present unity of being. If man has been able to raise himself from the '*the unrest of the accidents of life*' because he is one who has been able to assume death and been able put death into work. One can quickly point out the *phallocentric* figure of the onto-theological metaphysics in the figure of the worker: the onto-theo-logical figure of the worker as always that of a man, who after passing the mere disparate existences, been able to redeem his existence into the concentrated *whole,* who *works* and *produces* history by putting negativity into labour.

This universality which the individual *as such* attains *is pure being, death;* it is a state which has been reached *immediately,* in the *course of nature,* not the result of an action *consciously done.* The duty of the member of the family is on that account add this aspect, in order that the individuals ultimate being too, shall not belong solely to nature and remain something irrational, but shall be something *done,* and the right of consciousness be asserted in it... death is the fulfilment and the supreme 'work' which the individual as such undertakes on its behalf. (Hegel 1998, p. 270)

It is Antigone's brother who makes this passage from the elemental unconsciousness of the nether world, which is his 'supreme work' of death and not Antigone herself. She is one who is outside the state while still inside, a private individual being, the singularity of the 'remaining', the indifferent difference to the universal. The woman is the unconscious night of immediate existence whose law is in nether world of fury of the elements. She is the one who is *yet* to sublate herself into the universal *work* of the state. As such she is non-figure par excellence, an excess. This excess is the excess of pain that knows no consolation in the universal, public institutions of political reason. Her mourning is also a protest against the tyranny of the universal reason. As such, she is the excess of the state, the remnant at the limit of totality of significations of speech, the outside of the historical discourse of the world; she is the remnant of mere *scream* against which the state must pass judgement through its work of law, for through this work of law, through its terror that the state *is*. Yet, she is also the one who performs the last duty of the universal, by burying the dead body of her brother so that his death would not be a natural death of the animals but through death, freed from his sensuous existence he would a find a place in the community.[6] She has 'the highest intuitive awareness of what is ethical'(Hegel 1998, p. 274) and yet she is not conscious of it. Woman as such is

> ...An internal enemy – womankind in general. Womankind—the everlasting irony (in the life) of the community—changes by intrigue the universal end of the government into a private end, transforms its universal activity into a work of some particular individual, and perverts the universal property of the state into a possession and ornament of the family... the community, however, can only maintain itself by suppressing this spirit of individualism, and because it is an essential moment, all the same creates it and moreover, creates it by its repressive attitude towards it as a hostile principle. (Hegel 1998, p. 288)

Woman is "*irony*" because she is excessive in relation not only to the community in which individual finds his place through the negating action of death (community which she manipulates through her intrigue), but also in relation to herself. She does not belong to the community *enough* because she does not belong to herself: such is the strange nature of her existence as "private" being. Therefore it is she who possesses the danger to the universality of the state power, to the universal order of reason. She is the excessive negativity, an infinite mourning for her brother, a cry of the night that *un-works* the community, or any aspiration towards the formation of totality of significations. As *mere existing*, she poses threat to the law of the state, for her irony seeks to empty out and undermines in advance the ontological ground of the community; she is *differance*, the 'bad infinity' of forever deferring and differing excess, which cannot be sublated once and for all. That's why "irony" is dangerous, unforeseen deliverance of reason to its own unworking, the ruse that transforms the universal order into mere *private* use; she is dangerous because, unable to sublate herself into the 'human law' of the universal signification, yet she claims to fulfil the work of reason and truth.

It is Antigone, then, who is a tragic figure, the 'everlasting irony of the community. Irony, therefore, subverting and threatening the very work of negativity, threatens to throw the community to its bottomless abyss, to its vertiginous groundlessness. Irony is the unworking of the universal order of political reason. If the onto-theological community finds its emblem in the figure of the worker which is always male (the Name of the Father), this subject of community always confronts the opponent in the figure of the woman, the irony that undermines in advance the universal order of the faceless reason. What is important here is to notice that Hegel had a glimpse into what is truly tragic, in the character of Antigone: her irreducible excess, her irony and the negativity that she represents, the unworking unconsciousness, the night that threatens to deliver all foundational gestures of Reason into a vertiginous abyss. Already foreshadowing Nietzsche's "unconsciousness" as tragic and the irony of the tragic philosopher, Hegel discovered Antigone as unconsciousness of the community itself, the surplus of the universal order, and the danger of the tragic as the unworking irony. But this truly tragic is immediately domesticated, as in Hegel as much as in Aristotle. Instead, the speculative use of tragedy employs it for the service of *Aufhebung*; what is *Catharsis* for the one, for the other it is Absolute Concept. Like in Plato but without his harsh judgment, it is finally the tragic that seems to be the 'internal enemy', which should be destroyed or subsumed at any cost so that the essence of community be preserved. The meaning of the 'world' be saved and the work of negativity can pursue its movement to its utmost conclusion. For Hegel, it is war that subsumes this 'internal enemy' (Hegel 1998, pp. 288-9).

This war is the war to arrest the excess of negativity, the internal wound of the negative who is Antigone. As always, Hegel gives a place to its own excess in his discourse but this excess would not be pushed to the limit. It is not affirmed to the limit but only to the extent that it preserves the "whole" all the more firmly, so that system is conserved from an excessive expenditure of mourning. Antigone's mourning over her brother would soon be cut short by waging a war against her "irony", against her excess and subduing her singularity by the other power of the negative: her irony would be made to feel the power of the negative by the other irony, the dialectical irony that saves the universal work of Reason by allowing the community to scream, at its very limit so that scream would be sublated into speech. Antigone feels the 'power of the negative' and subsumes herself to the universal order of Reason, for in this dialectical logic, irony must be nullified by far more unforeseen irony; the violence of the fury must be annihilated by another law-posting work of violence. This constitutes her sacrifice on the basis of which community maintains itself. As such the reappropriation of what is excessive, the scream of the feminine, and the tragic takes the form of speculative tragic knowledge, the catharsis of *Aufhebung*. Antigone acknowledges that she has erred and this acknowledgement is her tragic wisdom. What thus appears as Antigone's tragic knowledge is the resolution of the dialectical contradiction in which the excess of negativity is recuperated again and is reduced to the dialectical moment within totality. The whole of dialectical paradigm is this representation of negativity—the sublation of the individual, private subject to the universal, public subject of philosophy. Through the work of death, the human not only learns to scream but also speak. This *logos* of the political is essentially public by virtue of its universality. Its logic is the sacrificial logic of language. It is on the basis of this work of death, on the profit of speech that sacrifice delivers that an anonymous, total order of Reason is determined to be founded.

Death must work. This is tragic essence of the metaphysics of the political. For a long time the metaphysical determination of community founds its inner essence in this work of death, on the dialectical paradigm of sacrifice and war as essentially tragic reappropriation of the limit and it excess. This metaphysics, after all, is metaphysics of sacrifice and representation of its violence. It recognizes that all the sources of the human community, all ideals of human truth, the foundation of the human community must pass through the anguish of sacrifice and the vanishing away of voice. What Hegel sought through *Antigone* is to represent this anguish dialectically. He exploited tragedy speculatively to conserve what is sheer annihilation through the power of negative. At the end, tragedy has turned out to be only a comedy show, the sure return of the same through his death that is already guaranteed in advance. Hegel's pre-supposition-lessness has remained is its presupposition. This presupposition is that in the sublation of *voice* into *speech*, of private into public, nothing essential would be lost and nothing outside will remain. What has thereby remained unaccounted is the death of the other who would not return as Subject of history. The other is the un-sacrificiable only because only the other can be and is sacrificed and all the time. The death of the other alone is unproductive and whose death alone is produced for the sake of the *logos* of the political. The cry of the other is neither voice nor speech, neither "private" nor "public": it is the immemorial lost presence that alone makes the logos of the political possible.

If the ethical order determines tragedy as dialectical representation of the work of *Aufhebung*, the work of war against the singularity of the Other (whose death the survivor mourns), it is therefore made necessary that the universality of judgment in the name of which Creon undertakes to exercise the work of law on singulars, should be put into question. This judgment must arrive not in the name of "private" (the other is not private), but beyond any "private" and "public"; such a judgment is inseparably bound up with the idea of justice to the other. The death of the other does not belong to the dialectical tragic knowledge, and is excess of the law positing violence[8] in the name of speech. The cry of the other resonates at the limit of speech, as if from infinity, for all the time to come, for all that time that has elapsed and that would not return. Such a cry is the incessant grief murmuring without *logos*. It is an endlessly finite limit, one that is not determined as dialectical. It means neither "private" nor "public". Outside these distinctions, the other is the immemorial outside.

## Notes

1. Who more than Nietzsche has this profound insight that it is violence that constitutes community, that the very instituting of community—community that determines the possible non-violent co-existence of the members and the sharing of existence, the distribution of the essence of the community—this act of instituting already assumes violence, violence of making law and command as imperative for the community, for the maintenance of itself as whole.

   Nietzsche writes: 'In the act of cruelty the community refreshes itself and for once throws off the gloom of constant fear and caution. Cruelty is one of the oldest festive joys of mankind. Consequently it is imagined that the gods too are refreshed and in festive mood when they are offered the spectacle of cruelty- and thus there creeps into the world the idea of the voluntary suffering, self chosen torture, is meaningful and valuable' (Nietzsche 1997, p. 17). I would have liked to dwell on this complex relationship between tragic representation, which is based on the idea of sacrifice and the emergence of national community. Walter Benjamin, while distinguishing mytho-poetic tragedies from immanent historical Truerspiel, traces the emergence of tragic representation and its complex relationship to the community to the idea of sacrifice. Benjamin thus writes, 'Tragic poetry is based on the idea of sacrifice. But in respect of its victim, the hero, the tragic sacrifice differs from any other kind, being at once a first and a final sacrifice. A final sacrifice in the sense of atoning sacrifice to gods who are upholding an ancient right; a first sacrifice in the sense of the representative action, in which new aspects of the life of the nation becomes manifest. These are different from the old, fatal obligations in that they do not refer back to a command from above, but to the life of the hero himself; and they destroy him because they do not measure up to the demands of the individual will, but benefit only the life of the as yet unborn, national community. The tragic death has a dual significance: it invalidates the ancient right of the Olympians and it offers up the hero to the unknown god as the first fruits of a new harvest of humanity' (Benjamin 1998, pp. 106-7).

2. Thus war is what the community assumes for preventing its internal private spheres to be immersed in its isolated, finite existence and thereby preventing fragmentation that destroys the Whole: War on behalf of the community's maintenance is thus maintenance of this whole. Thus Hegel writes: 'War is the spirit and the form in which the essential moment of the ethical substance the absolute freedom of the ethical self from every existential form, is present in its actual and authentic existence. While on the one hand, war makes the individual systems of property and personal independence, as well as the personality of the individual himself feel the power of the negative, on the other hand, this negativity is prominent in war as that which preserves the whole' (Hegel 1998, pp. 288-9).
3. 'Death, if that is what we want to call this non-actuality, is of all things the most dreadful and to hold fast what is dead requires the greatest strength... but the life of Spirit is not the life that shrinks from death and keeps itself untouched by devastation, but rather the life that endures it and maintains itself in it. It wins its truth only when, in utter dismemberment, it finds itself. It is this power, not as something positive, which closes its types to the negative, as when we say of something that it is nothing or is false, and then, having done with it, turn away and pass onto something else; on the contrary, Spirit is this power only by looking negative in the face and tarrying with it' (Hegel 1998, p. 19).
4. 'This contradiction which being-for-self must resolve that of the disparity between its being-for-self and the state power is at the same time present in the following form. That renunciation of existence when it is complete, as it in death, is simply a renunciation; it does not return to consciousness; consciousness does not survive the renunciation, is not in and for itself, but merely passes over into its unrecognized opposite. Consequently, the true sacrifice of being-for self is solely that in which it surrenders itself as completely as in death, yet in this renunciation no less preserves itself. It thereby becomes in actuality what it is in itself, becomes the identical unity of itself and of its opposite self' (Hegel 1998, p. 308).

5. 'But essence that is in and for itself, and which is at the same time actual as consciousness and aware of itself, this is Spirit' (Hegel 1998, p. 263).
6. 'The dead individual, by having liberated his being from his action or his negative unity, is an empty singular, merely a passive being for another, at the mercy of every lower irrational individuality and the forces of abstract material elements, all of which are now more powerful than himself: the former on the account of the life they possesses, the latter on the account of their negative nature. The family keeps away from the dead this dishonouring of him by unconscious appetites and abstract entities, and puts its own action in their place, and weds the blood relation to the bosom of the earth, to the elemental imperishable individuality. The family thereby makes him a member of a community which prevails over and holds under control the forces of particular material elements and the lower forms of life, which sought to unloose themselves against him and to destroy him' (Hegel 1998, p. 271).
8. Such thinking, however, is not unimaginable. I am thinking here of Walter Benjamin's notion of politics of 'pure means', un-mediated non-violent resolution of human conflicts, beyond any mythic or law positing violence. This paper points towards such thinking, thinking that has remained to be thought: with this question of violence in relation to *law* and *justice*, as one can see, is ineluctably bound up the enormous questions of human freedom and the possibility of evil in the world. I refer to Benjamin's discussion of violence and its complex relation to law and justice (Benjamin 1979, pp. 132-54.)

# *The Tear of Reading*

Responding once again to the Heidegger-Sartre debate, I attempt here to think the question of finitude anew in its essential relationship with freedom as otherwise than the question of Being or of human Subject, otherwise than nothingness or negativity, but as an infinite responsibility, ethical in that, to the other and to the other's finitude. This ethical responsibility interrogates not only the project of 'fundamental ontology' that Heidegger sets himself in *Being and Time* (1962), but also the metaphysics of subjectivity that Sartre didn't radically put into question in his *Being and Nothingness* (1966), whether this metaphysics of subjectivity is thought as phenomenological ontology, or as onto-theo-logy in Hegelian dialectical-speculative philosophical discourse. This demands that the question of freedom needs to be thought anew in relation to finitude, not only of the other, but the finitude of the very philosophical discourse itself.

Ontology has merely enabled us to determine the ultimate ends of human reality, its fundamental possibilities, and the value which haunts it.

—Jean-Paul Sartre (1966, p. 784)

Every humanism is either grounded in metaphysics or is itself made to be the ground of one. Every determination of essence of man already presupposes an interpretation of being without asking the truth of being, whether healingly or not, is metaphysical. The result is that what is peculiar to all metaphysics, specifically with respect to the way the essence of man is determined, is that it is 'humanistic'.

–Martin Heidegger (1978, p. 202)

## I

Hegel reportedly once said: *mended socks are better than the torn ones, so says common sense, but not so with consciousness* (Heidegger 2003). Consciousness must 'suffer violence at its own hand', so it goes in *Phenomenology of Spirit* and it 'spoils its own limited satisfaction' (Hegel 1998, p. 51). Therefore, philosophy can only be a 'way of despair' (Ibid., p. 49), when consciousness is torn asunder. It is as if philosophy as the infinite recognition of its own infinity can only be something like God suffering mortality by looking death face to face in all its power of negativity. Yet this 'suffering of finitude' must also be redeemed, for consciousness is no mere 'tarrying with the negative' (Ibid., p. 19) but rather a calligraphy of death, a work of death which is the source of all human ideals and meanings. Here lies the redemption and justification of humanity, in the *Aufhebung* of infinite self-recognition and of mortal opening to the Absolute.

So must be reading and writing. Wringing is the absence of the finite subjectivity of the philosopher of flesh and blood, of Hegel who likes pretty girls and wine, suffers bankruptcy and has a bastard child. Writing rather delivers the writer to the work of death, allowing the mortal flesh and bones be consumed. Writing, above all philosophical writing bears the mark of sadness of finitude. Even animals are sad, so Gods too! Otherwise would God have created the world? Thus thinks Schelling (1936). There is, as it were, a deep melancholy at the very ground of existence. Schelling thus says that the world would not have come into being if there were no melancholy, albeit as mere potentiality, at the ground of the creator's existence.

So writing is connected to death. Hegel has died when writing *Phenomenology of Spirit*, while still being alive, as if, death itself exists in him in a manner as if life no longer matters. Hegel 'suffered violence at his own hands', hands that hold pen and white paper and releases writing. The movement of death is the movement of negativity. But we readers, arriving always after him, after his funeral is over, reads his death in his writing. Now his death acquires a sudden, brilliant, lucid presence never occurred before, which is the very possibility of meaning, of a life after death, redeemed and transfigured intelligible being. Hegel suffers at his own hands, and is resurrected in our hands, reader's hands, by reading himself through our reading of him. The second Hegel is identical and different to the first one. The second Hegel is reparation of himself, reparation of the tear that is opened by the *spacing* of his writing. The torn sock of consciousness needs reparation. For moments the tear of the system opened itself to the brilliant lucidity of the night, but is repaired very soon, closed once again, affirming the closure of the sovereignty of the Subject.

Is it not that the tears of the other exceed all presence-absence of a philosophical *Eros* of reading and writing? Is it not that the mourning over the other's death beyond repair, and therefore refuses the intelligibility of an auto-engendering being? Such an infinite mourning for the other must forever open the closure of being, beyond the intelligibility of self-presence, beyond its calligraphy of death, beyond the power of the negative and beyond the unity of the concept. Reading and writing that imperceptibly delivers us, transports us—not to my death, but to that of others, always others—such infinite mourning for the other's death would not be mended, but would remain inconsolable, a wound that would forever overflow the total order of cold, anonymous reason. Tears are always for the other even before it is for "me"—the tears of reading, reading that opens to the other in an infinite affection that "undoes" me, disrupts the continuum of my self-satisfaction and self-glorification.

There is thus no "proper" reading as such, reading that would be "property" of the reader or author whereby the intelligibility of the other (or "myself") may be guaranteed. It is rather that reading that infinitely responds to the other's finitude, mourns without being completely interiorized and sublated into self-consciousness. Reading refuses the "propriety" and "property" that is at one's disposal. Reading can thus only be non-proper. The diachrony of reading, because the reader is always later to arrive, refuses to grant the reader the power of memory to be able to recount its time of reading. The reader is always non-contemporary in relation to himself and thus *already* exposed to the other before *coming* to oneself. Responsible, philosophical criticism of "adequate" and "inadequate reading", "right" and "misreading", important though these concepts are and scientific or objective they may appear to be (wherever their scientificity lies), must always already appeal (but this is not regulative principle) to the non-proper of reading. It must attend to the tears and wound of reading addressing to the other who has already passed by or who is yet to be born. Responsibility to the other thus always appears to be non-proper and inadequate, born before "me" and persisting after "me". Such is this travail of reading. The condition of possibility of reading is this non-propriety and non-property of reading; in other words, it involves us in the intrigue of an *impossibility* of reading. This does not mean that one must not read. It is rather otherwise: one must read—which means, one must always respond to the other—which makes, simultaneously, reading impossible, which means reading always fails, ineluctably, *always already non-proper*. The philological-scientific category of "right reading" and "misreading" does not found the possibility of reading, but they are founded upon this *non-propriety* of reading that ungrounds itself, unfounds while founding the possibility of "right reading" and "misreading". Each time there occurs reading, there is *already* affirmed the very impossibility of reading, the tear of reading. Without this, the Other would be reduced to the intelligibility of being, which would amount to be a sovereign assertion of the Same that assumes the right to death, to put death into employment for the sake of meaning and sense. *Beyond the violence of reading founded upon the work of death, there must already be opened another reading, beyond mastery and beyond violence, as infinite mourning, with prayers and tears for the other.* The philological-scientific formalist criteria of "good" and "bad" reading, in its concern of semantic-syntactic adequacy is not primordial. They already appeal to the primacy of a certain dominant concept of reason and intelligibility, and smells of mastery under the guise of something called "objective" and "neutral" meaning.

One must not renounce, however, the intelligibility and the work of reason but precisely to be affirmed in the name of responsibility to the other without reducing it to the intelligibility of being's mastery. This is not to say that all reading has to be affirmed. This is only to say that the question *which* reading to be affirmed—this is already not, what some say as 'relativism'—cannot be exclusively determined in the name of an intelligibility which the dominant philological discourse presupposes, but in it that it must affirm, which means it must *respond* to the finitude of the other, a reading that responds to the alterity of the infinite other. This means that it does not, and it must not amount to a founding of the concept of reading on some ontological principle of intelligibility.

## II

Did Sartre misread Heidegger? Posed the question of Sartre's supposedly "misreading" of Heidegger in this manner, this "misreading" is made to appear like an accidental tear in Sartre's System that wanted to constitute a *phenomenological ontology*— for we know, *Being and Nothingness* is thought to be a *phenomenological ontology*—so that the accidental "misreading" can be repaired by responsible philological or etymological criticism, whatever name one gives it. That was not, however, Heidegger thought that is at stake. Heidegger's response to Sartre's 'existentialist humanism' lies not in that Sartre misread him, but rather in this": that Sartre's determination of man, which presupposes certain determination of the relationship of man and being is precisely that must be deconstructed. It is here that one must raise the debate between Sartre and Heidegger. All questions of alleged "reading" and "misreading" must take into consideration what is at stake here, namely, how do we—as responding to the debate of Sartre and Heidegger—respond to the question of "man" (which is the question of the finitude of man), the relationship of man and Being, and (we will soon see) the question of freedom? How do we respond to this question: the question of the finitude of man as the question concerning what Heidegger and Sartre in different ways call "existence"?

Without much ado, let me bring into focus what is stake. The immediate context is that of Jean Beaufret's raising certain questions concerning Sartre's address *Existentialism is a Humanism* (in the following translation which I will be quoting, it appears as *Existentialism and Humanism)* where Sartre says,

> ... There are two kinds of existentialists. There are on the one hand, the Christians, amongst whom I shall name Jaspers and Gabriel Marcel, both professed Catholics and on the other the existentialist atheists, amongst whom we must place Heidegger as well as the French existentialists and myself. What they have in common is simply the fact they believe that *existence comes before essence.* (Sartre 2001, p. 27)

What makes Sartre say that Heidegger believes 'existence comes before essence'? In *Being and Time* there occur these lines, which Sartre must have read:

> The two characteristics of Dasein which we have sketched the priority of *existentia* over *essentia* and the fact that Dasein is in each case mine (*die Jemeinigkeit*)- have already indicated that in the analytic of this entity we are facing a peculiar phenomenal domain (Heidegger 1962, p. 68).

Yet in *Letter on Humanism*, the text we are considering, Heidegger's response to Sartre's 'existence preceding essence' consists in saying that because *ek-sistence* is 'ecstatic dwelling in the nearness of being', it is 'in fundamental contrast to every *existentia* and "existence" (Heidegger 1978, p. 222) and therefore—and this is important:

> Sartre expresses the basic tenant of existentialism in this way: Existence precedes essence. In this statement he is taking *existentia and essentia* according to their metaphysical meaning, which from Plato's time on has said that *essentia* preceded *existentia.* Sartre reverses the statement. But the reversal of a metaphysical statement remains a metaphysical statement. With it he stays with metaphysics in oblivion of the truth of Being (Ibid., p. 208).

And further,

> Concealed in its essential provenance, the differentiation of *essentia* and *existentia* completely dominates the destiny of Western history and all history determined by Europe... the basic tenet of "existentialism" has nothing at all in common with the statement from *Being and Time* (Ibid., pp. 208-9).

Thus Gilles Deleuze is right to say 'it involved no misunderstanding, since Sartre did not set out to write a commentary on Heidegger' (Deleuze 1994, p. 64). What Deleuze is discussing here is Heideggerian "nothing" which Heidegger attempts to distinguish from and also deconstruct (in Heideggerian sense of 'destruction of ontology') 'negativity', 'negativity' which precisely Sartre takes as point of departure for the task of constituting a *phenomenological ontology*. That means (which Deleuze does not disagree; in fact Deleuze's task is precisely to think, in *Difference and Repetition)* a *non-dialectical and non-negative difference* that must be able to take into account the Heideggerian 'ontological difference', for 'ontological difference' is seen by Heidegger as a *step back* from negative difference, and also from speculative difference. This means that Sartre's negativity is subject (this is what Deleuze recognizes in the same sentence) to Heideggerian 'destruction of ontology'. This should not lead one to suppose that I am making Deleuze anymore Heideggerian than Sartrean. This rather comes from my recognition that Deleuze's non-negative difference is not 'ontological difference' at all and that it is no longer the question of being for Deleuze, but the question of *sense*, as Deleuze explicitly says in his review of Jean Hyppolite's *Logic and Existence.*[1] What Heidegger was saying in the above paragraph is (as Deleuze discusses) that Sartre's existence has nothing to do with what Heidegger calls *ek-sistence.* It is thus not a matter of commentary here, though Sartre himself (as we saw above) in his *Existentialism and Humanism* explicitly refers to Heidegger's 'existence preceding essence' as atheist existentialism. Thus it is not the question of mere mistranslating or so called "misreading" that what Heidegger argues against Sartre, for that would amount to claim that Sartre wanted to say that same thing, because he is commenting on Heidegger but said in the wrong way. Heidegger is rather saying that Sartre said a different thing, nothing at all the same, because Sartre is not merely commenting. Therefore the question would not be resolved at all by reading "correctly", but rather in the fact that what Sartre says and presupposes in saying 'existence precedes essence' is itself what needs to be interrogated in the first place. The debate between Sartre and

Heidegger is not the mere the matter of philological misreading, mistranslating. Therefore, even when one grants that Sartre did not misread/mistranslate Heidegger, if there such a thing exists, Heidegger's critique would still remain to be taken into consideration. Otherwise it is mere matter of some sort of philological or etymological concern and nothing more than that, which evades what is at stake, namely, 'how to think man'? Heidegger's critique operates, thus, in showing *difference* in differentiating *Existenz* as *ex-sistence* from "existence" of atheistic existentialist humanism. This is already otherwise than a question of mere mistranslation. Let us read Heidegger as closely as possible here.

What is it to say, *The essence of Dasein lies in its existence* (Heidegger 1962, p. 67)? Heidegger explains this as follows:

> The 'essence' (*Wesen*) of this entity lies in its "to be" (*zu Sein*). Its Being-what-it-is (*was -Sein*) (*essentia*) must, so far we can speak of it at all, be conceived in terms of its Being (*existentia*). But here our ontological task is to show that when we choose to designate the being of this entity as "existence (*Existenz*), this term does not and cannot have the ontological significance of the traditional term "*existentia*"; ontologically, *existentia* tantamount to being-present-at hand, a kind of being which is essentially inappropriate to entities of Dasein's character. To avoid getting bewildered, we shall always use the interpretative expression "presence-at hand" for the term "*existentia*", while the term "existence" as a designation of Being, will be allotted solely to Dasein. (Ibid)

It is in this sense Heidegger's saying 'existence comes before essence' is not mere reversal of metaphysics; yet it is Sartre's saying of the same words is interpreted by Heidegger as mere reversal of metaphysics. This means: Dasein's *Existenz* is *otherwise* than "*existentia*" and "*essentia*", while the latter, which is *presence-at-hand* (*Vorhandenheit*), as distinguished from *Existenz*, presupposes *Existenz* and remains oblivious of *Existenz*. In so far as "existence" is determined as "subject"[2], producing and produced—which always presupposes the metaphysical determination of "man" as autochthonous producing one "existence", thus determined, is *presence-at-hand.*[3]

This means that in Sartre's determination of "man" as "producer" (this determination running from *Being and Nothingness* to *Critique of Dialectical Reason*[4]) the metaphysics as metaphysics of labour has remained unquestioned. It is in this sense Sartre's notion of the "subject" remained onto-theo-logically metaphysical, despite Sartre's desperate attempt to distantiate from Hegelian philosophy. It is here one must place the question of negativity and nothingness, and it is in this context we have to understand Heidegger's contention with Sartre.

However, the place of Hegel is extremely complex issue. Sartre's reading of Hegel, even when he attempts to distantiate himself from Hegel, remains influenced by Kojeve's anthropocentric reading of Hegel, whose lecture Sartre attended. His "Hegel" remained Kojevian and none but that. The post-Sartrean critical response, including his contemporary Merleau-Ponty's last works, to Sartre's notion of "subject" and "freedom" has to do with entirely new reading of Hegel. This change has to do with Jean Hyppolite's formidable critique of Kojeve. It is to Hyppolite that all of them (Foucault, Derrida, Deleuze[5]) are indebted for a non-anthropocentric reading of Hegel, seeing there the possibility of deconstruction of the "subject" and the question of deconstruction of philosophy itself.

Thus Sartre's reading of Hegel's *Phenomenology*, following Kojeve, ignores that *Phenomenology of Spirit* is supposed only to be introduction to the system, and that a phenomenology also occurs in *Encyclopaedia,* which is Hegel's system, in the third part in the *Philosophy of Spirit*. Here, as Derrida rightly points out (1982)—and we certainly do not need Derrida to point it out —that "phenomenology" is a stage already sublating "anthropology" as the truth of man which is other than "man". This means that phenomenology is not 'anthropocentric' at all. As the truth of man, phenomenology is already sublation of "anthropology". In this sense "man" as producer, in its inseparability with the notion of "subjectivity"(this idea remained uninterrogated by Sartre, but rather Sartre himself determines "man" to be such, as late as *Critique of Dialectical Reason)* remains open to Hegelian dialectical critique itself.

## III

Thus Sartre's existentialist humanism is a certain determination of "man" which remains metaphysical in its critique of the very metaphysics. It is this determination of "man" that led Sartre to determine freedom in relation to "decision" as much as the concept of the Subject. The Subject of freedom which exists without anything proceeding as its ontological ground, must decide out of its sheer nothingness. This experience is what Sartre calls "anguish": 'That is what "abandonment" implies, that we ourselves decide our being. And with this abandonment goes anguish' (Sartre 2001, p. 35).

Freedom is the anguish of decision. This decision, without *substantia* and *essentia* as its metaphysical ground, is always the decision "to be". Here freedom, which is freedom "to be" at the same time, with its evocation of a certain notion of "action" whose metaphysical determination Sartre never interrogates (a concept whose metaphysical determination goes as far as Aristotle's distinction of *potentia* and *actualitus*), is freedom determined as "possibility". This possibility of freedom is, with Heidegger too, always 'possibility of all impossibilities' (Heidegger 1962, p. 262), whether it is question of the "subject" or "being". I would not quote Heidegger whose phrase the above is, but Sartre:

> There is no other universe except the human universe, the universe of human subjectivity. The relation of transcendence as constitutive of man (not in the sense that God is transcendent, but in the sense of self-surpassing) with subjectivity (in such a sense that man is not shut up in himself but forever present in a human universe)—it is this that we call existential humanism. This is humanism because we remind man that there is not legislator but himself; that he himself, thus abandoned, must decide for himself... (Sartre 2001, p. 45)[6]

Whether it is Heideggerian *Being-towards-death* which in its ecstatic affirmation of its finitude asserts its freedom "to be" as its very *Abgrund* (which is freedom as 'possibility of all impossibilities'), or it is Sartre's humanist Subject in *abandonment* which must assert its freedom "to be", freedom is always determined, as in Hegel in relation to finitude as "possibility" (in the sense of "capacity") inasmuch as finitude itself is determined as "possibility", whether in Heidegger's 'possibility of impossibility' or in the humanist Subject's virile assertion of its own effective production wherein the metaphysical concept of "work" remained unquestioned (in Sartre). While in Heidegger the overcoming of metaphysics (metaphysics with its humanism and its onto-theo-logical determination of work, in innermost inseparability with subjectivity) is accomplished only in the name of existence (which is 'possibility of all impossibilities'); Sartre's critique of the very same metaphysics, with its privileging of *essentia,* is accomplished in the name "existence" understood as "humanism" with its privileging of human subject, from which the thought of freedom is thought. In this way, the insistence "to be"—whether humanist or non-humanist—remained sovereign which in its turn determines the question of our finitude and its relation to the whole question of freedom only as *capacity.*

In this sense, the question is that of finitude. Whether finitude is understood as *nothing* or as *negativity,* finitude always appears as that must be "possible"—a capacity or a power. Western philosophy remains singular in the manner that it uniquely profits from death. Death is understood as *possibility* of all meaning and source of all ideals, as *possibility* of the very discourse that constitutes for us a totality of significations. This death or finitude is always the abyssal source of the freedom "to be", freedom of the one for whom its finitude is at stake, inasmuch this finitude is possible for it as the very possibility of its freedom "to be". This dominant discourse knows no other death, no other freedom other than the virile assertion of its right "to be". *Finitude has always been determined, in this dominant discourse, only either in relation to Being or subject. 'Only Dasein can die, or only man is capable of death, only for being death is possible'. In humanist—atheistic discourse it occurs as: 'only man is capable of death, he alone realizes his freedom out of his nothingness as his freedom, the freedom 'to be''.*

Is not death rather the limit of all possibilities, as Blanchot (1995, p. 70) says in response to Heidegger, death that is 'the impossibility of all possibilities'? Is not death always, even before my *being-towards-*

*death,* the death of the Other that haunts me which makes the coincidence of me with myself impossible? Is not freedom, even before the freedom "to be", always the freedom for the other[7] in which case, *perhaps* not to be called "freedom" at all. Whether *Existenz* is *ex-sisting,* or *existence* is *existential*—in their singular relations to *Nothingness* and *Negativity*—the death of the other remained unthought; at best the other appears only either as Being-alongside-others, or as '*we*' of 'intersubjective[8] that Sartre talks about. Perhaps the very notion of Being, or Subject needs to be rethought and along with it the understanding of finitude in relation to the question of freedom.

However, in the very last works of Sartre, there seems to be an attempt at liquidation of the "subject", though, as we know, humanist Sartre is not the only Sartre that there has ever been. I have in mind *Nausea,* where there occurs a virulent critique of humanism. Towards the end of life, Sartre recognizes the notion of "subjectivity" as "useless":

> So, in *Being and Nothingness,* what you might call "subjectivity" is not it would be for me today: the little gap in the operation by which what has been internalized is re-externalized as an act. Today, in any case, the notions of "subjectivity" and "objectivity" seem to me entirely useless. Of course, I may happen to use the term "objectivity" but only in order to emphasize that everything is objective. The individual internalizes his social determinants: he internalizes the relations of production... then he externalizes all that in acts and choices that necessarily refer us to everything that has been internalized. (Sartre 1972, pp. 102-3)

## IV

The whole complex problem of freedom is at stake here—freedom in relation to finitude and being, along with the questions of ethics and the limit of the philosophical discourse itself. One must be able to go through the entire history of modern philosophical determinations of freedom: Kant's transcendental freedom as regulative principle, Hegel's transformation of its through the speculative-dialectical determination of negativity and Schelling's critical response to Hegel wherein (in Schelling 1936) freedom is understood as *Abgrund,* the *abyss* of a melancholic freedom that cannot be grasped by the intelligibility of the concept. Herein occurs the deconstruction of the dominant concept of freedom, the dominant concept of freedom which always understands freedom as "possible" and "effective realization" through the negativity of labour inasmuch as Being is already determined as "possible". Though Heidegger's own understanding of freedom as *Abgrund,* in response to Schelling, attempts to *step back* from dialectical onto-theo-logy, it also remains, however, a freedom "possible" inasmuch as finitude—because it is the finite freedom for the "*Being-towards-death*"—itself is determined as 'possibility of all impossibilities'. I would have like to dwell on this question of freedom, taking my point of departure from Schelling's notion of melancholic freedom as *Abgrund,* which is outside all possibilities and impossibilities in order to develop an entirely other concept of freedom, in relation to an entirely other, the infinite other and to develop an idea of finitude, which is not the finitude of *being-towards-death* (Heidegger 1962, pp. 279-311) nor the *abandonment* of the *Subject* (to itself), but always finitude of the other, finitude beyond all notions of possibilities and capabilities, beyond the effective production through the labour of the negative. 'My' (non) relationship with the other is not that of Heideggerian other-alongside-being (he calls it *Being-alongside-Others* as "equiprimordial" moment that belongs to Dasein's existential structure), nor that of another subjectivity within the totality called "the world" with whom I co-exist intersubjectively (while abandoned alone to myself, in anguish), but rather this: "my" (non) relationship with the Other "is" only a (non) relationship to the Other's finitude, a tear in "my" system, *a torn sock which can never be mended* in concept. This *tear* must remain open in mourning. This condition in its unconditionality, as its *Abgrund,* is the condition of all possibilities of Subject's freedom. This freedom which gives being its freedom, and gives Subject's freedom in anguish, always comes from the other, the Other's finitude, as that which has already come by, lapsed beyond repair and yet, yet to come. The very awakening of being to itself already presupposes that something has already lapsed (Schelling calls it "that has been"), that a *tear* has *already always* opened in the very heart of the opening, at the very possibility of awakening, that the other has already come to pass be without return. Therefore being, in its possibility, is nothing but the mourning for this other's death.[9] This means that the realized- realizable, *possible* freedom has its outside which is not exhausted in realization and in possibility of being's freedom "to be". The possibility of Being's freedom "to be" is only the limited freedom, is already granted its possibility by a freedom coming from an entirely other, from an un-posited abyss of the infinite past which cannot be exhausted by any possibility and realization of it. Being's freedom "to be" is possible rather by the very violent negation of the other's freedom, the freedom of the other, to which in its very freedom "to be" is held obliged and responsible. The task of mourning for the other's death is essentially freedom beyond the humanist Subject's freedom to decide its own being as Sartre thinks, and beyond Dasein's preoccupation with its very finitude, for whom its finitude is at stake (because its death in each case is its proper own).

Perhaps one day I will be able to articulate this problem in far more lucid manner, given the preliminary stage of my research at this moment. At best one may recognize at this moment, to articulate in a very crude manner, the exigency of thinking freedom—not as a question of the relationship between man and being, nor Subject's relationship to its decision towards it being to whom primordially it is responsible—but freedom as coming from an infinite other, which demands that the question of finitude itself to be thought anew and its relationship to time. It demands that we think anew the problematic of mourning as the task, as an ethical responsibility to the other.

## V

I conclude with a reference to an essay, entitled "Conclusion: Sartre and the Deconstruction of the Subject", that appears as conclusion to the *Cambridge Companion to Sartre.* In the very beginning,

Christina Howells(Howells 1992, pp. 318-52) announces in a very prophetic manner, a 'return of the subject', reading Sartre in a manner of reading Sartre after Derrida. However, ironically (and one is at a loss not knowing how to respond to it), the writer has merely shown that what Derrida's deconstruction of "subject" (and Derrida deconstructs the "Subject"!) and 'the ends of man' amounts to be, Sartre has already accomplished a great deal. This shows merely the contrary of 'the return of the Subject' which is supposed to be the thesis of the essay. One does not need here even to mention about her oblivion of Derrida's deconstruction of a certain dominant metaphysics of "work" and its complex relations to the notions of "property" and "propriety". Yet these are the very motions that she locates in Sartre (which can be read in *Critique of Dialectical Reason,* the text from which I quoted in this paper) to show how Sartre deconstructs the humanist "Subject" in a manner not very far from Derrida, to which, according her, Derrida should have acknowledged. Yet these are the very notions that are taken up in Derrida's deconstructive strategy of reading. Perhaps it is a good time to take this problem anew: to think again what this supposed 'deconstruction of the subject' amounts to.

## Notes

1. See "Appendix: Review of Jean Hyppolite's (1997, pp. 191-6). This dense, brief text is extremely important for us to understand certain developments in the second half of 20th century French philosophy, that arises out of the exigency to respond to a certain reading of Hegel, a certain Hegel: Derrida's notion of differance, and Deleuze's non-representational difference are responses to this exigency of thinking non-negative and non-speculative difference, in which sense both these thinkers are indebted to Heidegger's critique of non-onto-theological metaphysics and Heidegger's ontological difference.
2. Thus Sartre takes as the point of departure Cartesian *cogito*, though distinguishing from Cartesian philosophy at another level, in that Sartre understands existence to be essentially intersubjective. Sartre says in *Existentialism and Humanism*: 'At the point of departure there cannot be any other truth than this, I think therefore, I am, which is the absolute truth of consciousness as it attains itself. Every theory, which

begins with man, outside of this moment of self-attainment, is a theory which thereby suppresses the truth, for outside of the Cartesian *cogito*, all objects are no more probable and any doctrine of probabilities which is not attached to a truth will crumble into nothing. In order to define the probable one must possess the true before there can be any truth whatever, then, there must be an absolute truth, and there is such a truth which is simple, easily attained and within the reach of everybody; it consists in one's immediate sense of one's self' (Sartre 2001, p. 38). Heidegger's' 'destruction of ontology', ontology which has assumed the form of metaphysics as history of beings, attempts to show how, through a reading of that history itself, determination of being as "subject" only arises in that history as transformation of *Ousia* into *Certitudo* (Descartes *cogito*), and in that sense, epistemological and *phenomenological-ontological* (including Husserl's transcendental ego) is nothing but metaphysical oblivion of the originary meaning of Being as *Aletheia* (Heidegger 1975). Sartre's critique of the essentialist determination of subject as essential does not deconstruct the history of the metaphysical determination of this concept called "subject" itself. Therefore Heidegger says, 'man is never first and foremost man on the hither side of the world, as a "subject" whether this is taken as "I" or "we". Nor is he ever simply mere subject, which always simultaneously is related to objects, so that his essence lies in the subject-object relation. Rather before all this, man in his essence is, ex-sistent into the openness of Being, into the open region that lights the "between" within which a relation of subject to object can "be" (Heidegger 1978, p. 229).

3. '*Dasein* does not have the kind of being which belongs to something merely present-at-hand within the world, nor does it ever have it. So neither is it to be presented thematically as something we can come across in the same way as we come across what is present-at-hand' (Heidegger 1962, pp. 68-9).
4. Thus in *Critique of Dialectical Reason*, Sartre refers to, 'the perpetually resolved and perpetually renewed contradiction between man-as producer and man as-product, in each individual and at the heart of each multiplicity' (Sartre 1960, p. 158). With this determination of "man as producer, the whole determination of "action" as "work", with its notion of property and propriety and history determined as the labour of the negative is at issue. Sartre's critique of dialectical reason presupposes and appeals to this determination, which has determined to be such in Hegel's *Phenomenology of Spirit* (as Kojeve reads this text).Therefore despite Sartre's distantiating himself from Hegel's onto-

theology, Hegel's determination of labour and negativity as the innermost essence of "man" has remained operative in Sartre's early phenomenological-ontology and latter in *Critique of Dialectical Reason*, in so far as *Being and Nothingness* takes negativity as point of departure (and Heidegger's puts into question) and *Critique of Dialectical Reason* still determines "man" as producer. In *Letter on Humanism,* Heidegger brings this innermost metaphysical determination of "man" as labour" in the following way:

'The essence of materialism does not consist in the assertion that everything is simply matter but rather in a metaphysical determination according to which every being appears as materials of labour. The modern metaphysical essence of labour is anticipated in Hegel's *Phenomenology of Spirit* as the self-establishing process of unconditioned production. This is the objectification of the actual through man experienced as subjectivity. The essence of materialism is concealed in the essence of technology' (Heidegger 1978, p. 22). In another place, Heidegger says, 'in order to be able to delineate more clearly the relations which carry the connection between "work:" and "pain" nothing less would be necessary than to think through the basic fundamental structure of Hegel's metaphysics, the uniting unity of the *Phenomenology of the Mind* and of the *Science of Logic*. The fundamental character is "absolute negativity" as the eternal force of reality, that is, of the "existing concept". In the same (but not the equal) belonging to the negation of the negation, work and pain manifest their innermost metaphysical relationship... if anyone, indeed, dare to think through the relationship between "work" as the basic feature of being and "pain" via Hegel's *Logic*, then the Greek word for pain, namely *algos*, first becomes articulate for us. Presumably *algos* is related to *alego*, which as an intensive of *lego* signifies intimate gathering. Then pain would be the most intimate of gatherings. Hegel's concept of the "concept" and its properly understood "tension" say the same thing, on the transformed level of the absolute metaphysics of subjectivity' (Heidegger 1959, pp. 70-71).

5. See Deleuze's review of *Logic and Existence*.
6. One must be able to determine the transformation of this notion of transcendence. Heidegger, taking into account of Sartre's Transcendence as "constitutive of man", understands that what he (Heidegger) considers as transcendence is otherwise than what is "constitutive of man", but as *ex-sisting* beyond man. Here Heidegger refers to this notion of transcendence in Being and Time, where it is

shown to be, not the "constitutive of man", but rather ex-sisting in so far as this transcendence is understood as "es gibt". ' Being and the structure of Being lie beyond every entity may posses. Being is the transcendence pure and simple' (Heidegger 1962, p. 62).

7. It is not a matter of decision—thus not of existential anguish—whether to respond to the call of the other's finitude or not, but responding to the other's finitude, that calls for my prayers and tears, precedes all decisions, let alone the decision for one's being.
8. Thus Sartre say, '...The intimate discovery of myself is at the same time the revelation of the other as a freedom which confronts mine, and which cannot think or will without doing so either for or against me. Thus, at once, we find ourselves in a world which is, let us say, that of "intersubjective" (Sartre 2001, p. 39).The transcendence of the other, in its very infinitude, would not appear as another "subjectivity" to a "subject" in an "intersubjective world" (wherein subject dialectically limit each other, everyone appearing as other to the other, and yet, in the name of very "subject" appearing as other, forms a 'we') nor alongside Being with beings—in as equiprimordial moment to outside the world as others-alongside-being. The transcendence of the other is not alongside Being nor another "subjects" of otherwise than the subjectivity of its other (s); but rather: it speaks already from an immeasurable height, a distance not as each limiting others freedom, but with tears of its finitude. This finitude is neither Nothing (of Being), not the Negativity of the "Subject".
9. Eternal freedom entails for thinking finite beings, according to Schelling, an *Abgrund*, a non-identity, which is 'terminus *a quo* of our thinking ... eternal freedom is the unthinkable, that which no one can think of as ever being, but eternally only as past/having- been (*Gewesen)*" ( Schelling 1969, p. 92). In the *Age of the World*, this "having-been" is thought as *Aground* of Absolute freedom, that conditions all possibilities of the effective realization of freedom, yet eludes the grasp of all grounding and all conditions: 'man learns that his peaceful dwelling place is built on the hearth of a primeval fire, he notices that even in the primal being itself something had to be posited as past before the present time became possible, that this past remains hidden in the ground and that the same principle carries and holds us in its ineffectiveness which would consume and destroy us in its effectiveness' [Schelling 1946, p. 13). This *Abgrund* is 'a region in which there is no ground at all but rather absolute freedom. The "unground" of eternity lies this close in every person, and each is horrified by it if it brought to his consciousness' (Ibid., 93).

# *The Logic of Sovereignty and Bare Life*

The essential task of Giorgio Agamben's *Homo Sacer: Sovereign Power and Bare Life* (1998) is to articulate the metaphysical foundation of the dominant political discourse in the West, discourse that is founded on the modality of the production of death which is inseparable from the production of bare life. This production of bare life, understood as of the one who can be killed, but un-sacrificiable—at once excluded and included, or better as *included exclusion*—secretly determines the metaphysical paradigm of the political. This ambivalence of the bare life that can be killed but not sacrificed, has its symmetrical structural counterpart in the notion of Sovereignty. Thus the notion of sovereignty implies the existence of bare life as authentic political existence. Drawing on the works of Carl Schmitt (2006) who understands Sovereignty as the state of exception, and sovereign as the one who decides on the state of exception, Agamben puts forward the thesis that the fundamental activity of the sovereign is none but the production of its structurally symmetrical counterpart, that is, production of bare life, for like the bare life, the sovereign at once belongs to the generality of the order of Law (for all positivity and conserving activity of law presupposes as the condition of its possibility the generality of the order) and yet, since he is the one to decide on the state of exception which is irreducible to the generality of the order who must not, for that matter, belong to that order. Thus the paradoxical logic of at once inclusion and exclusion, or the paradox of *included exclusion* that intimates both the production of bare life and the logic of sovereignty as the two-fold structural symmetry of Western politics. The inclusion of "life" in modern democracy as the calculable element where the essential task of politics is determined as what Foucault calls the 'right to life', does not refute the Aristotle's metaphysical determination of politics, which is of a political existence only as qualified life, "bio" as opposed to "zoe", but rather that modern democracy confirms it on a new understanding. Thus it is no longer the task of the political to "make death and let live", but its inverse, "make life and let die" which in its very inversion rather confirms the old metaphysical foundation of politics. Thus *Auschwitz* is not merely accidental, contingent historical event, but may be said to be the paradigm of Western politics as such, which in its metaphysical foundation is always already *bio-politics*, or rather a *bio-metaphysics.* If Western metaphysics is uniquely profited from death (that death must be a "work", the "most supreme work of death" as Hegel calls it in *Phenomenology of Spirit*[1]) then death, understood metaphysically in relation to production (which is for that matter metaphysics of work, this metaphysics of death) is the same as the production of bare life that can be killed but not sacrificed. *Auschwitz* only confirms it as the historical paradigm. Here then I summarize the basic three theses in Agamben's own words, which he has put at the end of his book. They are: '1. The original political relation is the ban (the state of exception as zone of indistinction between outside and inside, exclusion and inclusion). 2. The fundamental activity of sovereign power is the production of bare life as originary political element and as threshold of articulation between nature and culture, zoë and bios. 3. Today it is not the city but rather the camp that is the fundamental biopolitical paradigm of the West' (Agamben 1998, p. 181).

The three theses mentioned above constitute the provisional conclusions of the inquiry in *Homo Sacer*, part I, which is called "Sovereign Power and Bare Life". In part II, titled *States of Exception* (Agamben 2005), he is concerned with the contemporary condition of world politics. Grasping the essence of the contemporary modern political condition whose political task is determined as continuous maintenance of the states of exception so that continuously bare life may be produced, especially in big democracies like America, Agamben applies his provisional thesis on Sovereignty that he sets out in his first part. In Part III of *Homo Sacer*, titled *The Remnant of Auschwitz* (2002) he further elaborates the third thesis, that is, Camp as paradigm of the modern Bio-politics. In this text he articulates the questions concerning the very possibility and impossibility of testimony, and the complex relation between life and death, complicated by recent developments of medicine, where what is at stake is not mere neutral knowledge- production but the very *politicization* of death and life, of what is to be "human" and "non-human": the distinctions on the basis of which Western politics was based, have now entered into the 'zone of indistinction'. Thus Agamben inserts the figure of what is called 'muselmann' (which is otherwise than any figure, but rather its very existence, or non-existence calls into question the very possibility of "figurality" of "the figure") as the 'zone of indistinction' between human and non-human, made possible by *Auschwitz.* This makes impossible henceforth the distinction of human and non-human on the basis of which Western metaphysics of politics has been based. Thus what is called for is a politics no longer on the basis of the traditional distinction of human and non-human and between zoe and bio but radically otherwise. This *politics of the otherwise* he tries to think as the possibility of the pure potentialities not in relation to the being of actuality, or ontology of actuality, working on and therefore critiquing from Aristotle to recent linguistic theories, passing through Schelling's works, to think of a notion of potentialities which is not reducible, or radically heterogeneous to the metaphysical foundation of politics in its two-fold structural symmetry between *bare life* and *sovereign power*, where what operates in bare life and sovereign power the logic of *included-exclusion. The political thinking, which is also thinking of the political, must be otherwise than the logic of bare life and sovereign power.* But in which way the thinking of pure potentialities, not in relation to Being of actuality-will be radically heterogeneous thinking of the political is not clear yet, which is still awaited.

Given these theses which in no way may be thought to be exhaustive, but only a bare outline of *Homo Sacer*, I find the importance of Agamben's contributions as three-fold. 1. While drawing on Foucault's work on bio-politics who never thought the relation of bio-politics with sovereignty in any systematic manner, perhaps his early death prevented him, and on the other hand, drawing on Carl Schmitt's notion of Sovereignty as the state of exception, who never thought the relation of Sovereignty with bare life, Agamben thinks these two theses together as inseparable, symmetrical structure where the same logic operates, and founds the foundation Western politics. This is the most important contribution of Agamben. 2. The second contribution lies in the application of his first two theses: while *Auschwitz* remains the paradigm of the modern bio-politics, it is inseparable from the state of exception that is continuously maintained in modern democracies and therefore *Auschwitz* is not the only site, or place where bio-politics manifests its terrible face, but bio-politics remained continuously operative in our political existence, more intensely than ever before. Hence it is a naiveté to assume that bio-politics has ended with *Auschwitz*, rather it is a more terrible truth when the discourse that in the name of inalienable human right deconstructs the destruction of "life", it is the very sacredness, or unsacrificiability of bare life that is evoked in its very unsuspecting form of a critique. Thus it is in the application and elaboration of Foucault's (2010) notion of bio politics, taking *Auschwitz* as historical paradigm, and the application of Carl Schmitt's notion of Sovereignty in a critical way that Agamben contributes most significantly to understand the contemporary historical existence. If one of the lasting contributions of Foucault lies in the radically new way he has posed the question of power, that means power understood outside the juridico-political order, Agamben attempts to think the notion of sovereignty, already implied by Carl Schmitt, outside the juridico-political order, thinking sovereignty as more originary in its irreducible connection with the reference of law to life as the inscription of the later as state of exception in respect to law. Thus the question of sovereignty is no longer to ask: 'what is the superior force legitimatizing itself within the general order of validity and regularity of law and legality?', but to interrogate the originary structure when sovereignty, in order for the general order of law and legitimacy to be possible in reference to life, places itself outside the general order of validity and legitimation, and therefore outside the normative order of legality. It is the sovereign violence, in distinction from legal violence that constitutes the constituted order where legal violence may be possible. Thus while hitherto the critiques of violence calls into question the violence manifested within the constituted order of law, violence that is supposed to rule over life—in the way that 'human rights' activists speak of violence of law over life—Agamben finds these critiques insufficient in that these critiques don't call into question the constituting violence which is irreducible to the constituted power, irreducible to the *violence of law over life*. The critique of sovereign violence (sovereign violence which is the vanishing point, or "zone of indistinction" between the constituting violence and constituted violence) is irreducible to the juridico-political critique of violence, for the sovereign violence lies not in the application of law, but in the suspension of law for the application of law to be at all possible and therefore this suspension cannot be said to be "given". There is no given sovereign violence, but sovereign violence gives the possibility of the "given" order for the law to be possible. Therefore the juridico-political critique of violence also cannot account for modern bio-politics, any more than the distinction of sovereign violence and violence of the law, precisely because modern bio politics is marked by continuously sovereignty becoming rule or better, by entering into the 'zone of indistinction' of sovereignty and rule, nature and law. Third is the radically new way that the 'Auschwitz' question is posed, no longer merely in a historical way that investigates its cause in the historical condition, in a manner that Hannah Arendt analyses the rise of the great totalitarian states in the twentieth century. Agamben goes further: instead of analysing the "Auschwitz" question in the manner mentioned above, he discusses the metaphysical foundation of Western politics from Aristotle onwards, who understands politics metaphysically, that means on the basis of the distinction between zoe and bios. This means that the question of bio politics is not mere reducible to the historical comprehension, but one must be able to trace in its metaphysical determination. This is, despite drawing on Foucault's work, the profound departure from Foucault's manner of thinking. Thus, to distinguish from Foucault's manner of thinking, Agamben does not think the emergence of bio-politics merely in relation to certain historical conditions, that of emergence of modern state power where the zoe becomes included into political realm as the object of calculation of the state power. The point of biopolitics is not so much the inclusion of zoe into the political calculation of the state power, but entering into the 'zone of indistinction' between the two. This indistinction, not maintained by Aristotle, does not refute the logic of bio-politics but confirms it as becoming the very condition of modern bio-politics. While Foucault locates the emergence of modern bio-politics at that point when 'territorial state' passes into 'the population state', Agamben finds modern bio politics in the inseparable relation of bare life to sovereign power, when *physis* and *nomos*, life and law—whose link founds the sovereign power—threaten to become indistinguishable in so far as modern politics continuously maintains the state of exception. Therefore modern politics is immediately bio politics in a far more originary way than the power manifested in the prison and schools, for it is not concerned with the violence of the specific penal law that is possible within a constituted order of regulation and regularity, a regularity which the violence of law demands as its necessary condition.

It might be interesting to bring into discussion the point of disagreement and agreement with deconstructive gesture of thinking the political. Agamben argues that it is not so much the politics of friendship, based upon the distinction of friend and enemy that the Western thinking has its foundation, but far more complex paradoxical relation of bare life and sovereign power where the logic of included exclusion operates, which is the foundation of modern politics, which in the name of democracy may even align with great totalitarian powers. If the task of deconstructive thinking is to think the undecidable non-condition, the spacing of the event that is singular, Agamben finds this structural similarity with the state of exception which not belonging to the general order of the law and therefore belonging nor to the particular, is singular, by a necessary logic. This interpretation would have been violently rejected by Derrida, whose later works are devoted precisely to the deconstruction of the notion of sovereignty (Derrida 2006).[2] What is unfortunately not articulated in Agamben, who simply passes the question off in a hurried manner, that the notion of singularity in Derrida is precisely deconstruction of certain notion of decisionism that is inseparably bound with Schmitt's understanding of Sovereignty. *It is necessary to understand that undecidable is precisely the idea of non-sovereignty.* Another profound disagreement with Jean Luc Nancy is this: while Nancy thinks that the metaphysical determination of Western politics is the work of death, where death is determined on the modality of sacrifice, for Agamben, while agreeing with Nancy (2003) on the politicization of death as metaphysical foundation of politics, he disagrees with Nancy in that it is rather the bare life that is precisely who is unsacrificiable. Hence it is not the sacrificial modality of death that is the political foundation, but the unsacrificiability of bare life. Therefore the radical political task is not that of thinking the unsacrificiable, but to go beyond the logic of sacrifice as such, which any way (so Agamben claims) is made redundant in modern political state by the fact that contemporary political existence is marked by absence of sacrifice and sacrificial death. Therefore it is double irresponsibility of those who names with the name "holocaust" which has a certain connotation of sacrifice. This question has to be further examined, taking the political-philosophical discourses of the dominant tradition, especially Hegel's theologico-political discourse. What Nancy attempts to deconstruct is the sacrificial modality of death, and death determined as work that secretly operates in Hegelian onto-theo-logical discourse, where a political theology of death and its work governs the movement of the concept, and the dialectical process of history. One may be able to exhibit it while reading the crucial passages from *Phenomenology of Spirit*, not to talk about the

*Philosophy of Right* and other texts. This notion of sacrifice, which in Hegel's case understood in a Christian manner, intimates the dominant philosophical tradition. Deconstructive gesture of thinking attempts to think of the question of a death as heterogeneous to this tradition of sacrificial modality of thinking death, especially articulated in Hegel's onto-theo-logical determination of the political. This gesture of thinking runs from Heidegger to Blanchot, from Lévinas to Nancy: to think of a death that is *un-working* (Blanchot) or think of the death of the other (Lévinas), which is to think the non-negative dying, beyond the employment of death in service of universal history. The context where Nancy articulates this question is in relation to Bataille's critique of Hegel's negativity where (according to Nancy) the very same sacrificial modality of thinking operates. The point here is that for Nancy the idea of the un-sacrificial radically undermines Western political thinking. For Agamben, however, this unsacrificiable of the bare life is precisely to be questioned, since production of bare life is precisely the production of the un-sacrificiable. It is not to say that there should be more sacrifices, but to recognize that sacrifice is not *the* paradigm of death for Western politics. It is rather, so Agamben argues, the politics of bare life and logic of sovereignty.

The question that interests me (beyond the question whether death is determined in Western political metaphysics on sacrificial modality or on the unsacrificiability of the bare life) is this very place of death, its econo-mimesis of death that secretly operates in the dominant metaphysics and its complex relation to the theologico-politics. If one seriously takes into account Hegelian onto-theo-logical determination of death as sacrifice, which he thought as negativity, this is the moment one must see as the very foundational moment of Hegelian metaphysics. The task is perhaps to think the place of death beyond negativity. But how to think death otherwise, and thus neither on the modality of sacrifice nor unsacrificiability of bare life, this question is not yet addressed by Agamben. It is here thinking of both Lévinas and Blanchot help us to develop a sustained manner of interrogating the foundation of the theologico-political of metaphysics, which is therefore also a critique of ontology. A critique of sovereign violence and the production of bare life must be able to interrogate the theologico-politics of ontology. Thus both Lévinas and Blanchot saw that the task of thinking of the political in a profoundly new manner demands to think death itself otherwise than death on the modality of sacrifice. Despite Agamben's dwelling on the question of bio-politics, he strangely never dwells on the question of death in itself that secretly governs the theologico-political foundation of the West. Therefore the insufficiency of Agamben's interrogation of the place of death in its very metaphysical determination leads him to think language itself and language's relation to the non-linguistic, to its exteriority as none but a relation of suspension or as "negativity". Therefore language itself appears to Agamben as none but based upon the modality of negativity, that means language on the very basis of the logic of sovereignty. Agamben's thinking of language remains inscribed in the very theologico-politics that he attempts to deconstruct, as negativity, in the passage between voice and language, between *phone* and *logos* that founds bio-politics and is the secret source of all sovereignties. Discussing Hegel's notion of Language in *Phenomenology of Spirit*, Agamben could thus write: 'Language is the sovereign who, in a permanent state of exception, declares that there is nothing outside language and that language is always beyond itself. The particular structure of law has its foundation in this presuppositional structure of human language. It expresses the bond of inclusive exclusion to which a thing is subject because of the fact of being in language, of being named' (1998, p. 21). And in another place Agamben says, 'As the pure form of relation, language (like the sovereign ban) always already presupposes itself in the figure of something non-relational and it is not possible either to enter into relation or to move out of relation with what belongs to the form of relation itself' (Ibid., p. 50). Here the relation of language to the non-linguistic, or the non-relation of language to its exteriority is thought on the basis of negativity, and thus as sovereign ban, a relation that finds fulfilment in the onto-

in the onto-theologico-semiology of Hegel.[3] With Lévinas and Blanchot the relation, or non-relation of Language to the other is thus not the relation of constituted power to constituting power, or constituted power to the sovereign power, but it in its non-power, is a donation which is non-negative, and therefore that can not be thought on the basis of sovereign ban. The relation of language to the other, to the exteriority is not suspension, nor privation, nor negation, but non-negative opening, not as a "zone of indistinction" but an opening where donation that means giving is possible at all, as an impossible gift. This opening where gift is given precedes the negativity of the sovereign suspension, for negativity can only be thought on the basis of a circulation of powers, even when one talks of constituting power, or sovereign power as the "zone of indistinction". Beyond the circulation of sovereign power and constituted power, an opening has to be opened that may not be merely suspension or negation, but on the basis of an opening the negativity of the sovereign ban may arise. Thus language is to be thought far more primordially than on the basis of sovereign ban in order for the circulation of powers may open to the otherwise as gift, which is the very gift of language. Despite a critique of sovereignty and its structure of ban, Agamben never thought language otherwise than on the very basis of suspension and negation, on the very basis of state of exception which he otherwise criticizes. As a result Agamben's thinking of language remains circulated and closed within the economy of sovereign power and constituted power, between suspension of the rule and constituted order of regularity. An opening beyond the circulation of the powers is the promise of language, which is not negative, therefore not the privation of ban. It is towards this opening that Rosenzweig, Heidegger, Lévinas and Blanchot's thinking of language promises; this promise is not the promise of the Law, but otherwise than Law, for a promise does not need general validity and legitimation and therefore does not presuppose for its condition the suspension of the order of regularity.

## Notes

1. Thus in *Phenomenology of Spirit*, Hegel writes, 'The deed, then which embraces the entire existence of the blood-relation, does not concern the citizen, for he does not belong to the family, nor the individual who is to become a citizen and will cease to count this particular individual; it has as its object and content this particular individual who belongs to the family, but is taken as a universal being freed from his sensuous, i.e. individual, reality. The deed no longer concerns the living but the dead, the individual who, after a long succession of separate disconnected experiences, concentrates himself into a single completed shape and has raised himself out of the unrest of the accidents of life into the calm of simple universality. But because it is only as citizen that he is actual and substantial, the individual, so far as he is not a citizen but belongs to the family, is only an unreal impotent shadow' (Hegel 1998, pp. 269-70).
2. For Carl Schmitt's notion of decisionism and his friend and enemy distinctions, see Schmitt (2006, 2007).
3. Elsewhere, especially in the collection of his essays as *Potentialities* (Agamben 1999), Agamben attempts to open up the dimension of language beyond any predicative function to the "thing itself", that is, language in its pure taking place that is irreducible to any "this" or "that" entities to have taken place. It is the verbal resonance of the "pure taking" and its messianic intensity that cannot be reduced to the logic of sovereign ban.

# *Redemption Beyond History?*

Our contemporary world is marked by ineluctable aporias, ethical, between requirements that are incommensurable to each other: requirement of redemption beyond history, without violence and reification, of an affirmation of a coming that is not oriented towards a logically-dialectically-immanently determined telos; and requirement, on the other hand, that recognizes that there is no world outside the immanent-historical one, so that reflections and acts of realization may turn their gazes to a 'here and now', to the immanent historical becoming of the world with its own logic that should be grasped by the historical-philosophical reflection. The ethical aporias arise when thinking confronting the limit and closure of history experiences the necessity to affirm of a redemption in coming 'here and now', of a transcendence without transcendent, of a coming with a messianic intensity outside the dialectical-historical and yet also the demand that the historical world, founded by the labour of the negative, may not be renounced. Thus the demand arises to the affirmation of both, and never of an affirmation of either in-itself, at the same time without reducing and minimizing the contestation and incommensurable character of this double demand. What remains, thus, as the aporetic limit, is none but an infinite contestation, a political and ethics no longer belonging to the order of possibility, but an affirmation of impossibility, a political and ethical at the limit.

# I

*What it is to think at the limit? That is the question.*

What it is to think at the limit? This question may not presuppose that something called "limit" is given and is thus determinable. Therefore we also ask: why at all there arises the necessity to think the limit, or to think at the limit? Limit of what? Who is that being that asks the question of the limit? And we will see that this question is essentially aporetic: limit delivers us to the necessity or an imperative to affirm what is impossible. That means: affirmation must traverse through the limit, or better, may we be traversed by the limit so that there may be affirmation. *Profound affirmation arises precisely at the limit when affirmation does not belong to the order of possibility.* We will say, provisionally to begin with, that aporia is that which does not belong to the order of possibility. The word "possibility" has acquired a meaning in our contemporary philosophical discourses besides what we immediately take it to mean, when, for example, one says: 'it is possible that cancer will be made to vanish from the world with the development of medicine'. From Heidegger onwards, the word "possibility" has acquired a new meaning: capability, or capacity to be, *to be able to be.* Possibility, understood in the Heideggerian sense, is essentially ontological, affirmed at the limit as 'the possibility of impossibility', *to be able not to be.* Thus when we say 'at the limit of possibility', and aporia as the question of this limit, it is the Heideggerian problematic of possibility that is *under* question. Affirmation, traversing through the aporetic, must affirm what does not belong to the order of ontological possibility, or possibility of the ontological. Does this traversing of the aporetic movement (the voyage of saying 'yes', which for that matter, must even risk shipwreck) amount to the dilemma of having to choose given alternatives (which already presupposes that freedom must already be a possession of the one who chooses, which must be his capacity, that belongs to his innermost possibility to be the one to choose) ? 'To be or not to be: that is the question' – this dilemma belongs to the order of possibility, the ontological possibility, the very possibility to be free in so far as freedom is determined here to be the property of the "human". In the dominant metaphysical discourse the question of freedom is always addressed as if freedom belongs to the property of being "human". May it not be otherwise: that "man" is called forth by a freedom whose inscrutable ground he cannot fathom and appropriate? This will mean: *man has a relation to a condition that is outside of him, that is otherwise than himself, a relation to a ground outside of his possibility, one that is not the dilemma of 'to be or not to be'.*

What we have come to understand as aporia, albeit provisionally, which is otherwise than dilemma (understood as the freedom as property of the "human") as this: *that "the human" whose ex-sistence is in relation to a condition outside of all appropriation and all presence, he whose relation to a coming to presence demands an affirmation that is required of him, is always an affirmation outside of his possibility.* It is an affirmation, traversing through a pathway of the aporetic, which is the affirmation of the event of pure future, opening to what is *not yet* and to what does not belong to any appropriation and recuperation. One to whom what comes to him does not belong to him as his "capacity" is a *finite being.* Only in so far as man is finite that there is for him there is a promise of the event of pure future, one that is redemptive, opening him to infinitude of what is yet to come from the very heart of his finitude. He must affirm out of his essential finitude—that means at the limit, at the limit of his possibility—what is always *coming,* not "this" or "that" coming but *coming itself, coming as such* that would not come to pass away. We should now reformulate what we initially said that aporia is that which we must affirm the impossible, that we recognize the necessity and imperative to affirm what "cannot" be affirmed. We now say: *we always affirm—at the limit —precisely because we are finite, affirm what we cannot appropriate to our capacity and what does not belong to our mastery and appropriation.*

Man is that who, insofar as he is essentially finite, has a relation to an impossibility that he must affirm. And he must affirm what is *yet to come;* he must affirm a future of affirmation and an affirmation of future. That is his redemption. Only an affirmation of coming redeems him, redeems the whole of his unredeemed history, a history (effectuated and produced out of the violence and labor of the negative, that belongs to his possibility, the very possibility to be "human") that requires a *coming* outside of itself, outside of the negative labour of history. How to think of a *coming* that is not exhausted in what is arrived? *As if a certain transcendence or eternity has withdrawn from the historical time of the world, and thereby keeping the promise of the arriving of an otherwise.* This wholly otherwise does not unfold along with the unfolding of the homogeneous, successive movement of historical time. It does not accompany, without disrupting, the great historical process of the becoming of the world. It does not coincide with the effective presence that defines the immanent politics of self-presence. By withdrawing from the total order of immanent self-presence, it may welcome *the world to come*, opening the *polis* to its future which is a surprise - *polis* with its melancholy of violence, with its festivity and sports, the harvesting and the laughter of the new born. What has already come in the world has not thus saturated the world yet; the world has not yet fully actualized the unconditioned potentiality of its promise. Rather a cadence of melancholy, arising out of the unredeemed claims of the earth is still heard, arriving from the near nearer than any self-presence and from a remoteness of an immemorial past.

This question, however, is not unique to the last and this century, though it is felt most urgently now than ever, when death (when so many concentration camps taking place every day) no longer appears in its existential dignity, and the capacity to be "human". It rather evokes the limit of the historico-political determination of existence, and the necessity to affirm an outside of this process, an unconditional affirmation beyond any historical totality and closure. This limit is now visible, more than ever before, in the task that modernity imposes upon itself, which is that of actualizing and realizing the ideal of certain historical existence without any transcendental ground in the name of a "reality" that must be rendered rational here and now. This has precisely made possible, in philosophical tradition of thinking, the emergence of German Idealism, especially the Hegelian version of Idealism that must unify *actus* and being in one principle of mediation. This transformation of Kantian transcendental thinking into the dynamic becoming of the historical world with its own immanent logic in Hegel's speculative-dialectical thinking gives itself precisely this historical task: that ideals must be realized and actualized here and now; that presence must present itself, essence must make itself existent, so that ideals may not remain mere yearning of the beautiful soul and so that nothing remains as mere poetry of the ineffable. The poetic ideal which in its mere potentiality is also impotentiality must be translated into the sober prose of the absolute realization. Only then the hunger of the Spirit will be fulfilled. The tremendous importance of Hegelian philosophy, further intensified in Marx, for the entirety of 200 years lies precisely here: the task of thinking itself, in Hegel's hand, is neither contemplation of the beautiful, nor positing of a transcendental ideal of Reason which can only be infinitely approximated (as in Kant, or even in Fichte). Mere yearning makes what is yearned for impossible to be reached. Therefore is the necessity of the historical task to make present what is to come, *here and now*. The result is fascinating: *with Hegel, a historical here and now effaces all traces of transcendence, and the historical world* is conceived to be needing of no outside, a well-ordered world complete in itself, without remainder, harmonious and coherent. What thus can't be thought in the Hegelian discourse of totality the event of pure future that cannot be predicated in the regressive-immanent movement of the dialectical-historical becoming of the world, for the immanent—regressive re-capitulation of historical-dialectical thinking can only predicate what has been (*Gewesen*). Existence, in its very historicity, thus, feels the requirement of a future whose predication is not given in advance, so that it affirms what attunes it to the innermost depth: the messianic hope for an arriving redemption *here and now.* Since the world's be-coming is not yet finished, it must already be opened to such an absolute event of an incalculable arrival, since 'to think is to venture beyond' (as Ernst Bloch remarks), undertaking the adventure of thought in messianic ecstasy of hope for that which alone redeems the emaciated history crying aloud under the curse of violence. Hence is the aporia:

on the one hand, necessity to assert the labour of the negative, to make present what comes to be, to realize in self-presence through the power of the objective and through rational institutions that define our politics and history; and then, on the other hand, there arises another demand incommensurable to the former, the necessity of redemption of this history itself, the necessity of an affirmation beyond and otherwise than negativity, otherwise than what has been already realized, the necessity that what is *to come* may not be exhausted in what is realized. The aporia here is the aporia between, on one hand, the demand of a language of reason and negative; and on the other hand, the requirement of an affirmation otherwise than a reduction of reason to instrumentality at the disposal of the power of the dominant; the aporia between the demand of a history that must actualize the promise of the world that has an infinite potentiality, and the demand of a certain a-historicity, certain transcendence and eternity of an unconditioned that must exceed all representation in reason, that exceeds the very dynamic of a historical reason, withdrawing from such a reason in the name of being faithful to an absolute demand of an absolute fulfilment.

This dehiscence, this caesura, this abyss of heterogeneity between requirements incommensurable to each other, renders all thinking aporetic: thinking recognizes, on the one hand, the absence of transcendent entities outside the historical-immanent one; yet thinking also requires, for its own redemption, a transcendence of an ethics which is irreducible to politics, to the historical task of labour, in so far as critical reflection at all to be possible, there must already be an opening beyond what has already been. As if, as it were, thinking itself must respond to the double, aporetic demands of time. Thinking must gather, through recollection, the gallery of images that the speculative memory of history has collected while passing through the historical movement of the world-historical becoming; yet on the other hand, thinking must infinitely open itself to what has never been recollected in history, what has fallen outside it since time immemorial and what is yet to come. On the one hand thinking must forever preserve in memory the founding moment of the world so that it may take its flight only at the dusk; on the other hand, thinking must constantly interrupt what has already been given so that thinking, overcoming all that has become, must herald, in thunder and lightning, the coming murmur of the Dawn. There is a necessity to affirm what, by an ineluctable logic, the impossibility to affirm the other—dusk when the owl takes its flight, or lightening of the Dawn—for their very non-coincidence makes alone any affirmation possible. Hence comes impossible demand: to affirm this very impossibility itself, this aporia itself as the very condition of possibility of an ethics and politics, of redemption and history, of an affirmation and negation—both at the same time, in their very heterogeneity and difference. The necessity to affirm two languages when each one excludes the other lies in this: without redemption, without an affirmation of coming beyond the given, without an opening outside the historical, there manifests the most terrible evil—the evil of totality itself, when the self-presencing immanence of the *polis* refuses its very condition of possibility; on the other hand, redemption without history is an empty dream, or a sheer coming indissociable from an annihilation without remainder. Redemption requires a moment of its realization so that what is *to come* comes *here and now*; and yet a coming *to come*, it must at each moment exceed any historical 'here and now'. History in its immanent closure, in its totality without remainder reduces all ethics into law-positing and law preserving violence that defines the realm of politics. *Not to exhaust the domain of the political in the eternal circle of law-preserving and law-positing violence, it is necessary to open the political realm of conditioned realization to the ethical affirmation of the event of pure future, messianic in its intensity, that forever keeps the world open to the unconditional.* Therefore is the necessity to affirm of a messianic future outside any thetic violence, a justice outside law, transcendence outside the force and power of the negative. The task of thinking the later is the very task of thinking that Schelling's later philosophy undertakes. If there is a demand of positive philosophy, it is because violence of the negative has remained unredeemed and that requires an affirmation outside the regressive process of dialectical-historical closure, without renouncing the task of the negative, however. A critique of violence (Benjamin 1986) requires that which is without violence, that is without law-positing and law conserving violence, of what Benjamin paradoxically calls 'divine violence'. Divine violence, which is otherwise than violence, is messianic coming of redemption, the affirmation of which requires the un-incorporation of an un-predicable temporality within the historical-dialectical process of becoming the world.

The aporia of the contemporary philosophical thinking turns towards a meditation on time and death. Could thinking have been satisfied in the mere flight of the owl of Minerva, or to recover the founding moment of origin through infinite potentiality of regressive reflection, the historical world would not have had the requirement of lightening flash of the messianic justice. If the reason of the world from Hegel onwards has been determined to be that of a historical reason, it thereby has come to confront its very limit that comes in the form of a demand of a time *to come* outside the closure of historical reason, in-dissociable from each other in their very heterogeneity. As if thinking will henceforth be (has it ever been otherwise?) heterogeneous to itself, always being-in-excess and forever unsaturated. This heterogeneity is the very mark of affirmation from which thinking will henceforth, as it has been, be the measure of its limit that will always *un-measure* itself.

## II.

*What is it to think at the limit? That is the question.*

To think at the limit is to experience the double, aporetic demands that are made on it: it is to affirm a certain madness – that means a certain impossible relation to the event of pure future. The force of reason realizes the necessity that the impossible must be made possible, the unspeakable must be spoken, the unnameable to be named, so that not only one must speak the spoken, but must speak even silence, let alone whistle it. But there is another demand: that everything that is spoken, everything that is named, everything that is possible must be pushed to the limit, to the point when speech and the name becoming trembling, remain outside all speech, outside all names and all possibilities of the human speech. There is a demand that everything must be present and not mere longing; there is another demand that there may remain a future outside all presence and all that is past from which all presencing and past take the measure of a meaning. *Hence is the demand: the historico-political must make possible that which does not belong to the order of possibility, which it does so by interrupting its own immanence infinitely, since only the promise of the messianic redemption keeps alive the movement of history, in the manner that justice alone makes judgment meaningful, and that the unnameable alone makes the name to come out of itself. To recognize the dignity of this infinity is the very dignity of the act of naming itself with which the discourse called philosophy is primarily concerned.*

# *Bibliography*

Agamben, Giorgio, *States of Exception*, trans. Kevin Attell (Chicago: University of Chicago Press, 2005).

Agamben, Giorgio, *Remnants of Auschwitz: The Witness and the Archive*, trans. *Daniel Heller-Roazen* (Zone Books, 2002).

Agamben, Giorgio, *Potentialities*, trans. Daniel Heller-Roazen (Stanford: Stanford University Press, 1999).

Agamben, Giorgio, *Homo Sacer: Sovereign Power and Bare Life*, trans. *Daniel Heller-Roazen* (Stanford: Stanford University Press, 1998).

Aristotle, *The Basic Works of Aristotle*, ed., Richard McKeon (New York: The Modern Library, 2001).

Barth, Karl, *The Epistle to the Romans*, trans. Edwyn C. Hoskyns (Oxford: Oxford University Press,1968).

Bataille, Georges, "Hegel, Death and Sacrifice" and "Letter to X, Lecturer on Hegel" in *The Bataille Reader*, ed. Fred Botting and Scott Wilson (Oxford: Blackwell, 1997), pp. 279-300.

Benjamin, Walter, "Theologico-Political Fragment" and "The Critique of Violence" in *Reflections*, ed. Peter Demetz (New York: Schocken, 1986), pp. 312-3 and pp. 277-300.

Benjamin, Walter, *One Way Street*, trans, Edmund Jephcott and Kingsley Shorter, (London: NLB, 1979).

Benjamin, Walter, *The Origin of German Tragic Drama*, trans. John Osborne, (London and New York: Verso, 1998).

Benjamin, Walter, "The Concept of Criticism in German Romanticism" in *Selected Writings*, Vol. 1: 1913-1926, ed. Marcus Bullock and Michael W. Jennings (Cambridge and Massachusetts: The Belknap Press, 1996)

Benjamin, Walter, "Theses on the Philosophy of History" in *Illuminations*, trans. Harry Zohn (New York, Schocken Books, 2007, rprt), pp. 253-64.

Birault, Henri, *Heidegger et la pensée de la finitude* (Revue internationale de philosophie, 1960).

Blanchot, Maurice, *The Writing of the Disaster,* trans. Ann Smock, (Lincoln: University of Nebraska Press, 1995).

Blanchot, Maurice, "The Athenaeum" in *The Infinite Conversation*, trans. Susan Hanson (Minneapolis : University of Minnesota Press, 1993), pp. 351-9.

Blanchot, Maurice, *La Communauté Inavouable* (Paris: Les Editions de Minuit, Paris ,1983).

Bloch, Ernst, *The Principle of Hope,* trans. Neville Plaice, Stephen Plaice and Paul Knight (Cambridge and Massachusetts: The MIT Press, 1995), Vol. 1.

Chrétien, Jean-Louis, *The Unforgettable and the Unhoped for,* trans. Jeffrey Bloechl (Fordham: Fordham University Press, 2002).

Deleuze, Gilles, *Difference and Repetition*, trans. Paul Patton (London: The Athlone Press, 1994).

Derrida, Jacques, "The Ends of Man" in *Margins of Philosophy,* trans. Alan Bass (Chicago: University of Chicago Press, 1982).

Derrida, Jacques and Anne Doufourmantelle, *Of Hospitality*, trans. Rachel Bowlby (Stanford: Stanford University Press, 2000).

Derrida, Jacques, " Violence and Metaphysics" in *Writing and Difference,* trans. Alan Bass (London and New York: Routledge, 1978), pp. 97-192.

Derrida, Jacques, *Specters of Marx: The State of the Debt, The Work of Mourning and the New International* (New York: Routledge, 1994)

Derrida, Jacques,'" On Forgiveness" in *On Cosmopolitanism and Forgiveness,* trans. Mark Dooley and Michael Hughes (London and New York: Routledge, 2001), pp. 25-60.

Derrida, Jacques, *The Politics of Friendship*, trans. George Collins (London: Verso, 2006).

Foucault, Michel, *The Birth of Biopolitics: Lectures at the College de France, 1978-79*, trans. Graham Burcell (Palgrave and Macmillan, 2010).

Foucault, Michel, "Language to Infinity" in *Aesthetics, Method and Epistemology*, ed. James D. Faubion (The New Press, 1999), pp. 69-88.

Hegel, G.W.F., *Outline of the Philosophy of Right*, trans. T.M. Knox (Oxford: Oxford University Press, 2008).

Hegel, G.W.F., *Phenomenology of Spirit,* trans. A.V. Miller (Delhi: Motilal Banarsidass, 1998).

Hegel, G.W.F., *Logic*, trans. William Wallace (Oxford: Clarendon Press, 1975).

Heidegger, Martin, "Appendix IV: Davos Disputation Between Ernst Cassirer and Martin Heidegger" in *Kant and the Problem of Metaphysics*, trans. Richard Taft (Bloomington and Indianapolis: Indiana University Press, 1997), pp. 193-207.

Heidegger, Martin, *Being and Time*, trans. John Macquarrie and Edward Robinson (New York: Harper and Row, 1962)

Heidegger, Martin, "On the Question of Being", in *Pathmarks*, trans. William McNeill (Cambridge: Cambridge University Press, 1998), pp. 291-322.

Heidegger, Martin, *On the Way to Language*, trans. Peter Hertz (HarperOne, 1982).

Heidegger, Martin, *What is Called Thinking*? trans. J. Glen Gray (Harper Collins, 2004, reprint).

Heidegger, Martin, *Four Seminars*, trans. Andrew Mitchell and Francois Raffoul (Indiana: Indiana University Press, 2003).

Heidegger, Martin, "Letter on Humanism" in *Basic Writings*, ed. David Farell Krell (London and Henley: Routledge and Kegan Paul, 1978).

Heidegger, Martin, *The End of Philosophy*, trans. Joan Stambaugh (London: Souvenir Press Ltd., 1975).

Heidegger, Martin, *The Question of Being*, trans. Jean T. Wilde (London: Vision, 1959).

Howells, Christina, "Conclusion: Sartre and the Deconstruction of the Subject" in *Cambridge Companion to Sartre* (Cambridge: Cambridge University Press, 1992), pp. 318-52.

Hyppolite, Jean, *Logic and Existence*, trans. Leonard Lawlor and Amit Sen (Albany: State University of New York Press, 1997).

Kierkegaard, Søren, *Concluding Unscientific Postscript*, trans. Alastair Hannay (Cambridge: Cambridge University Press, 2009).

Kojeve, Alexander, *Introduction to the Reading of Hegel: Lectures on the Phenomenology of Spirit*, ed. Allan Bloom and trans. James H. Nichols, Jr. (Cornell: Cornell University Press, 1980).

Lacoue-Labarthe, Philippe, *Typography: Mimesis, Philosophy, Politics*, ed., Christopher Fynsk (Stanford, California: Stanford University Press, 1998).

Lacoue Labarthe, Phillippe and Jean Luc Nancy, *The Literary Absolute: The Theory of Literature in German Romanticism*, trans. P. Bernard and C. Lester (Albany: SUNY Press, 1988).

Lévinas, Emmanuel, *God, Death and Time*, trans. Bettina Bergo (Stanford: Stanford University Press, 2000).

Löwith, Karl, *Meaning in History: The Theological Implications of the Philosophy of History* (University of Chicago Press, 1957).

Manjali, Franson, "Time, Language and the Destruction of Power" in *Journal for Cultural Research*, Vol. 13, numbers 3-4 (London: Routledge, 2009), pp. 297-307.

Nancy, Jean Luc, *The Inoperative Community* (Minneapolis: University of Minnesota Press, 1991).

Nancy, Jean Luc, *A Finite Thinking* (Stanford: Stanford University Press, 2003).

Nietzsche, Friedrich, *Daybreak,* trans. R.J. Hollingdale (Cambridge: Cambridge University Press, 1997).

Nietzsche, Friedrich, "On the Uses and Disadvantages of History" in *Untimely Meditations*, trans. R.J. Hollingdale (Cambridge: Cambridge University Press, 1997a), pp. 57-124.

Plato, "Symposium" and "Apology" in *Selected Dialogues of Plato,* trans. Benjamin Jowett (New York: Modern Library, 2000).

Rosenzweig, Franz, *The Star of Redemption*, trans. Barbara E. Galli (University of Wisconsin Press, 2005).

Sartre, Jean-Paul, *Situations*, Vol. IX (Gallimard, 1972).

Sartre, Jean-Paul, *Being and Nothingness,* trans. Hazel Barnes (New York: Pocket Books, 1966).

Sartre, Jean-Paul, *Critique de la raison dialectique, precede de questions de methode, I.* (Gallimard, 1960).

Sartre, Jean-Paul, *Basic Writings,* ed. Stephen Priest (London: Routledge, 2001)

Schelling, F.W.J. von, *Initia Philosophiae Universae,* ed. Horst Furhmans (Bonn, 1969).

Schelling, F.W.J. von, *Die Welalter,* ed. Manfred Schroter (Munich, 1946).

Schelling, F.W.J. von, *Philosophical Inquiries into the Nature of Human Freedom,* trans. James Gutmann (Illinois: La Salle, 1936).

Schelling, F.W.J. von, *The Ages of the World,* trans. Jason M. Wirth (Albany: State University of New York, 2000).

Schelling, F.W.J. von, *System of Transcendental Idealism,* trans. Peter Heath (Virginia: University of Virginia Press, 1993).

Schlegel, Friedrich, "Athenaeum Fragments" in *Classic and Romantic Aesthetics*, ed. J.M. Bernstein (Cambridge: Cambridge University Press, 2003), pp. 246-60.

Schmitt, Carl, *The Concept of the Political,* trans. George Schwab (Chicago: Chicago University Press, 2007).

Schmitt, Carl, *Political Theology: Four Chapters on the Concept of Sovereignty,* trans. George Schwab (Chicago: Chicago University Press, 2006).

Spinoza, *On the Improvement of the Understanding, The Ethics, Correspondence,* trans. R.H.M. Elwes (New York: Dover, 1955).

Taubes, Jacob, *From Cult to Culture,* ed. Charlotte E. Fonrobert and Amir Engel (Stanford: Stanford University Press, 2010).

Taubes, Jacob, *Occidental Eschatology,* trans. David Ratmoko (Stanford: Stanford University Press, 2009).